TYPE 45 DESTROYER

2010 onwards

COVER CUTAWAY: **Type 45 destroyer.**

(Alex Pang)

Dedication

For my chum Ted, who was a great companion throughout the writing of this book, and continues to be so.

First published in 2014

Prof Jonathan Gates has asserted his moral right to be identified as the author of this work.

A catalogue record for this book is available from the British Library.

ISBN 978 0 85733 240 0
Library of Congress control no. 2013934883

Published by Haynes Publishing,
Sparkford, Yeovil,
Somerset BA22 7JJ, UK.
Tel: 01963 442030 Fax: 01963 440001
Int. tel: +44 1963 442030 Int. fax: +44 1963 440001
E-mail: sales@haynes.co.uk
Website: www.haynes.co.uk

Haynes North America Inc.,
861 Lawrence Drive,
Newbury Park,
California 91320, USA.

This book has been written using sources in the public domain and information provided by equipment suppliers. While every effort is taken to ensure the accuracy of the information given in this book, no liability can be accepted by the Royal Navy, the author or publishers for any loss, damage or injury caused by errors in, or omissions from, the information given.

Printed in the USA by Odcombe Press LP,
1299 Bridgestone Parkway, La Vergne, TN 37086.

TYPE 45 DESTROYER

2010 onwards

Owners' Workshop Manual

An insight into operating and maintaining the Royal Navy's largest and most powerful air defence destroyer

Jonathan Gates

Contents

BELOW HMS *Daring* in the Far East. *(Crown Copyright, 2013 L(Phot) Nicky Wilson)*

ABOVE HMS *Dragon* in the Arabian Gulf. *(Crown Copyright, 2013 L(Phot) Dave Jenkins)*

Acknowledgements

This book would not have been possible without the assistance of staff from the manufacturers and suppliers involved in the production of the Type 45 destroyer. I should like to acknowledge the many people who provided information and images used in the book: Geoff Russell (AgustaWestland); Peter Barrett (Airborne Systems); Hartwig Traut (Aljo); Keith Murray, Jeremy Close (Astrium); Adam Rang, Donna-Marie Matheson, John Fyall, Natalie Culver, Bill Cullen, Bob Moran, Carolyn Lang, David Downs, Dr Norrie McPherson, John Perry, Ross Mclure (BAE Systems); Johanna Probert (BMT Defence Services); Steve Kerchey (Chemring Countermeasures); Tim Wee (Cobham Mission Equipment); Peter Litchfield (CSD Sealing Systems); Chris Dillon (Dillon Aero); Jason Cross, Jim Mackintosh (FES Support Services); Mark Dannatt, Sarah Leach (GE Energy); Martin Eagle (Gullco International); Alan Virrill, Tom Powell, Tony Dimmock (Hamworthy); Carl Bookless (Johnson Controls); Conal Walker, Bethan Mason (MBDA UK); Tim Hinton (Northrop Grumman); Karen Bull, Tim Lilley (Pall Corp); David Abbott, Doug Palmer (Pellegrini UK); Rob Warne, Elspeth Levi (QinetiQ); John Eagles (Raytheon); Ian Ruddlesden (Raytheon Anschütz); Richard Partridge, Craig Taylor, Nigel Allen (Rolls-Royce); Dr Simon Benham, Ian Piper, Roger Wright (Selex); Kathryn Bell, John Warehand, Kieran Bustard (Thales UK); Mark Merrifield, Carol Doyle, Andy Davis, John Martin, Richard Lindsey (Ultra Electronics); Karina McCormack, Simon D. Howdle (Wärtsilä).

I am also indebted to members of the Ministry of Defence (Richard Bolwell, Neil Crozier, Wayne Curtis, Chris Evans, Nick Johnson, Steve Marshall); of the Royal Navy (Captain Mike Beardall, Commanders David Gordon and Simon Wallace; Lieutenant Commanders Lee Davies, Steve Hayton, 'BJ' Smith, Vince Owen and Jim Fraser). All helped with their expertise of Type 45 destroyers and the equipment fitted.

Special thanks go to the photographers mentioned in the captions who have allowed their images to be used. These thanks include Simon Owen of Airfix who allowed the use of some of the detailed photographs taken to produce model kits of the destroyers. I am indebted to Lieutenant-Commander Jonathan Pearce and members of his staff who took photographs especially for this publication. All other photographs are from official sources and I am grateful to those who helped unearth suitable images: Helen Craven (Head of Digital, RN); Neil Hall (MoD Defence Images); CPO Phot Tam McDonald (FPU(N)); Steve Saywell (RN Media Archive) and Patricia Summers (British Consulate-General: New York).

The book's visual impact has been particularly enhanced by the extremely detailed cover illustration and cutaways meticulously drawn by Alex Pang of MadBadMachines to whom I am very grateful. The illustration comparing the various destroyers is taken, with permission, from the work of enthusiasts mentioned who post their work on www.shipbucket.com. I am also grateful for the help of Fiona Starkey of Bath Design Centre for assistance with the diagrams.

On a more general note, I owe a great deal professionally to Peter Chamberlain FEng RCNC and the late Prof Louis Rydill FEng RCNC, who acted as mentors throughout my career and who selflessly imparted their knowledge, wisdom and enthusiasm for warship design.

I am grateful to my editor at Haynes, Jonathan Falconer, for the opportunity to contribute to this book about one of my favourite subjects. And, of course, my wife, Pam, for her continued patience and support.

Introduction

On 23 July 2009 HMS *Daring* was commissioned into service with the Royal Navy (RN) as the First of Class of six Type 45 anti-air warfare (AAW) destroyers. These complex warships incorporate several major advances in naval technology and are recognised as the most capable AAW vessels in the world. They will form the mainstay of the RN's fleet for the next three decades.

The project to design and develop HMS *Daring* began in earnest in 2000. The requirement, as articulated by the Statement of Mission Need, was for a warship that 'will be a versatile destroyer capable of contributing to worldwide maritime and joint operations in multi-threat environments, providing a specialist AAW capability until 2040'. This book will outline how this development was accomplished, explain its advanced technology and describe the formidable and intricate warship that was produced.

The six Type 45 destroyers represent a major enhancement in surface warfare capability and technology. They incorporate significant innovations that also anticipate technology

D32 HMS DARING
Launched   1st February 2006
Commissioned   23rd July 2009
Latin Motto   *"Splendide Audax"*
                         (Finely Daring)

D33 HMS DAUNTLESS
Launched   23rd February 2007
Commissioned   3rd June 2010
Latin Motto   *"Nil Desperandum"*
                         (Never Despair)

D34 HMS DIAMOND
Launched   27th November 2007
Commissioned   6th May 2011
Latin Motto   *"Honor Clarissima Gemma"*
                         (Honour is the brightest jewel)

D35 HMS DRAGON
Launched   17th November 2008
Commissioned   20th April 2012
Motto   *"We yield but to St George"*

D36 DEFENDER
Launched   21st October 2009
Commissioned   23rd March 2013
Latin Motto   *"Defendendo Vinco"*
                         (By defending I conquer)

D37 DUNCAN
Launched   11th October 2010
Commissioned   26th September 2013
Latin Motto   *"Secundis Dubusque Rectus"*
                         (Upright in prosperity and peril)

LEFT Badges of the Type 45 Class of anti-air warfare destroyers. *(Author/Crown Copyright Images)*

BELOW HMS *Daring*, the first of the class of Type 45 destroyers. *(Crown Copyright, 2010 LA(Phot) James Crawford)*

RIGHT Artist's
impression of two
Type 45 destroyers
in company with an
aircraft carrier, a
submarine and an
auxiliary vessel.
(BAE Systems)

required by other warships to be developed over the first quarter of the 21st century. Much of the equipment fitted to the destroyers represents technological advancements over the previous generation of warships. In particular two major original systems were developed specifically for the Type 45 destroyers: a radical new integrated electric propulsion system (IEPS) and Sea Viper, a state-of-the-art AAW system. Both of these revolutionary systems contribute to the superlative performance of the Type 45 destroyers.

HMS *Daring* is the first warship to feature an IEPS where traditional gearboxes are replaced with electric motors driving the propellers directly. The two gas turbine alternators (GTAs) powering the propulsion can create nearly 45MW of electrical power – sufficient to supply a city the size of Dundee. This system produces excellent acceleration, a very tight turning circle and a top speed of well over 27kt (50km/h). All this is achieved with noteworthy economy, giving the destroyer a range that would allow her to cross the Atlantic, carry out missions and return without refuelling. Alternatively, a Type 45 destroyer could sail from her home port to the Falkland Islands, a distance of 8,000NM (almost 15,000km), and arrive with fuel in hand. To complement the fuel capacity the destroyers can be provisioned for a 45-day mission in only 12 hours.

Sea Viper is the unique guided weapons system that provides the destroyer's AAW capability. This system includes the potent Sampson multi-function radar (MFR) that can simultaneously detect, prioritise and track hundreds of targets. The radar is so sensitive that it can detect at long range a target the size of a cricket ball and approaching at three times the speed of sound. Sea Viper can simultaneously fire multiple hypersonic defence missiles to neutralise several potential threats, guiding each of its missiles with high precision to a different target. The destroyers are capable of defending both themselves and task group forces over a wide area against a range of intense threats including a mass supersonic attack in which salvoes of missiles approach simultaneously from several directions in an attempt to overwhelm the fleet.

A warship's complex systems could not operate in harsh marine locations and potentially hostile military environments without its dedicated ship's company. This intricate fighting machine is also home to at least 191 men and women and may, at times, have to accommodate and sustain up to 235 personnel. The standard of accommodation is higher than any previous RN warship and provides a 40% increase in space per person relative to existing ships. Each member of the ship's company has their own berth in well-appointed cabins.

For the first time on board a destroyer, there are dedicated recreation spaces for all ranks and dedicated accommodation and facilities for additional personnel.

In order to provide an effective air defence capability over the warships' projected 30-year service lives, the destroyers have deliberately been designed with the flexibility to fit new equipment. Provision has been made to install identified systems that are already in service in other warships as well as those currently under development. This recognises the rapid pace of technological change and the need to allow for expansion if costly refits are to be avoided. The cost of the ship's hull, as against the complex systems it carries, is small; consequently a modest increase in ship size (and initial costs) is balanced against significant reductions in the cost of ownership. The result is a warship that has a displacement of about 8,000 tonnes, more than a third bigger than the class it replaces.

With a potent combat capability combined with high speed and extended endurance, Type 45 destroyers are proving to be robust, versatile, flexible and economic assets.

RIGHT The first four Type 45 destroyers in Her Majesty's Naval Base, Portsmouth: left to right HMS *Dauntless*, HMS *Daring*, HMS *Dragon* and HMS *Diamond*. *(Dan Grant)*

Type 45 key characteristics	
Displacement (light/ deep/design)	5,800/7,350/8,000 tonnes
Length overall	152.4m
Length waterline	143.5m
Beam	21.2m
Draught	7.4m
Air draught (height)	39m
Installed power	45MW
Top speed	> 50km/h (27kts)
Range	13,000km at 33km/h (18kts)
Endurance (end of life)	>13,000km (7,000NM)
Mission	45 days
Complement	191 (21 officers, 170 ratings)
Accommodation	235

ABOVE The Type 45 destroyers are longer than two Airbus A380s (the world's longest commercial airliner), almost as high as Nelson's Column and displace more than three Olympic swimming pools of water. *(Author)*

Chapter One

Development of the Type 45 destroyer

Developing the most potent warships ever built for the Royal Navy was always expected to be a challenge. Much of the constituent equipment was necessarily novel and developed in parallel with the ship. This included the unique, powerful Sea Viper missile system and the radical but economical propulsion system.

OPPOSITE *Dauntless* **on sea trials.** *(BAE Systems)*

The predecessors of the Type 45 destroyer

Like all warships, anti-air warfare (AAW) destroyers are expected to be able to perform a large range of military tasks. Their primary role is to protect groups of warships and their support vessels (such as a task force or battle group) against air attack from missiles and aircraft. They achieve this by using missile systems that can engage air targets at long range.

The true predecessor of the Type 45 destroyer could be said to be HMS *Bristol*, a Type 82 destroyer commissioned in 1973. She was fitted with a new AAW weapon, the Sea Dart missile system. HMS *Bristol* was to be the First of Class of four Type 82 destroyers whose main task would be to escort and defend task groups that would be led by the proposed CVA-01 large aircraft carriers. In 1966, while *Bristol* was being built, a defence review was carried out with the intention of cutting military spending. Although *Bristol* itself was spared, the Defence White Paper resulted in the cancellation of the aircraft carriers and, with a loss of their primary role, no further destroyers of the class were ordered.

There still remained the vital need to defend groups of vessels so a new class of much smaller destroyers, the Type 42, was built, the First of Class being HMS *Sheffield*, commissioned in 1975. To make significant savings in initial cost their size was constrained. They were barely large enough to accommodate their Sea Dart weapon system. The first batch of Type 42 destroyers was of six ships. The destroyers' small size meant that they were difficult and expensive to maintain, refit and upgrade. National endeavours to procure new designs failed, partially because building more Type 42 destroyers was always offered at a low initial cost. The UK was also involved in international design projects, but these proved costly and were each in turn considered not to be in the national interest. As a consequence, there followed two further batches of four Type 42 destroyers, each batch being slightly larger than the previous in order to accommodate minor capability improvements.

As well as their high cost of ownership, Type 42 destroyers were considered vulnerable, particularly because of the lack of a self-defence missile system to complement the long-range Sea Dart system. There was little protection against low-flying missiles launched close to the ship. This was demonstrated dramatically in the Falklands War. Furthermore, the class was short in relation to its beam and this resulted in poor sea-keeping characteristics.

Although they formed the backbone of the fleet for over two decades, by the end of the millennium the Type 42 destroyers were reaching the end of their operational life (designed to be 22 years). Sea Dart was also obsolescent and, as it could only engage two targets at a time, was unsuited

to protect against concerted attacks by the
latest threats. However, when HMS *Daring*
was commissioned in mid-2009, six Type
42 destroyers were still in service. They were
progressively paid-off as the new destroyers
replaced them. On 6 June 2013, the Last of
Class, HMS *Edinburgh*, was paid-off after 28
years' service.

Projects to replace the *Sheffield* Class Type 42 destroyers

There were six major projects to replace the
Type 42 destroyers before the successful
Type 45 programme was adopted.

In 1978 design work began on the first
potential replacement to HMS *Sheffield* Class
Type 42 destroyers, the Type 43 destroyer.
This class was to have two upgraded Sea Dart
systems (enabling it to defend against a more
concerted attack), two Sea Wolf self-defence
missile systems and Harpoon anti-ship missiles.
It was to operate two Lynx helicopters (against
HMS *Sheffield*'s single Lynx). The helicopter

A HMS *Bristol* Type 82 destroyer, the true
precursor of HMS *Daring* Type 45 destroyer.
(Mischa Campen)

B HMS *Sheffield* Type 42 destroyer, the class of
destroyers that was eventually replaced by the
Type 45. *(Mischa Campen)*

C The proposed Type 43 destroyer. *(Alan Alves)*

D The proposed Type 44 destroyer. *(David K.
Brown, Mischa Campen and Mike Ranson)*

E The proposed international NATO Frigate
Replacement for the 1990s. *(Martin Conrads)*

F The tri-national Common New Generation
Frigate (Project Horizon) that became the
Franco-Italian Horizon Frigate and contributed to
the Type 45 destroyer. *(Dr Rachel Pawling)*

G Photo of HMS *Daring* Type 45 destroyer for
comparison. *(BAE Systems)*

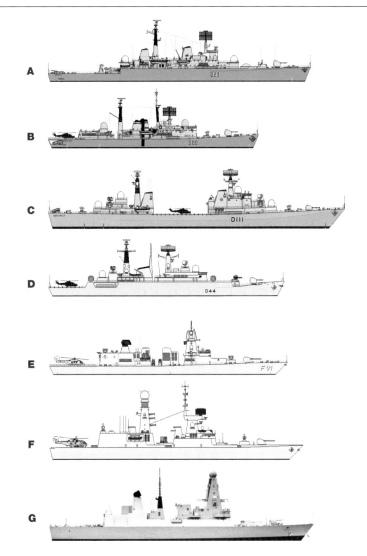

A *sandbag* was used both as ballast and as a silent anti-personnel weapon. Consequently when the UK's decision to leave the NFR-90 project was announced suddenly at the highest level it led to speculation that the project had been, not sandbagged, but *handbagged* by the Prime Minister, Maggie Thatcher.

JACKSPEAK

In the 1990s, several naval officers involved with, and frustrated by slow progress of, the tripartite *Horizon* project commented that the name was appropriate. However hard one struggles towards the horizon it never gets any closer.

deck was located between two superstructure blocks at the centre of the ship, where its motions were lowest. After four years' design work the Type 43 was abandoned as being too costly. Instead, an austere Type 44 was investigated. This was to be based loosely on the hull and propulsion system of the Batch II Type 22 frigate, HMS *Boxer*. Initial designs demonstrated that it would have most of the shortcomings of Type 42 destroyers, so the project was terminated. While a further replacement was sought, efforts were concentrated on improvements to Batch III Type 42 destroyers. These were lengthened in order to improve sea-keeping, so making them a more effective weapons platform.

At this time many NATO nations had similar requirements for AAW warships and this led to an ambitious programme by eight nations to develop the NATO Frigate Replacement for the 1990s (NFR-90). Although it was termed a frigate by most nations, it exhibited many of the features that, for the USA and UK, would categorise the warship as a destroyer. NFR-90 was to have a high degree of commonality, although from the start nations were free to choose their own AAW missile system from two contenders. As a consequence, the design was complicated by having to accommodate either a US-based or a French-led system. The selection of systems such as the anti-ship missile and even the choice of propulsion system were not common, thereby introducing even further complexity and cost.

Incompatibility with RN requirements, difficulties in reaching agreement on work-sharing, the inability to reconcile national variations of the design and the bureaucratic

complexity of project management all led to the UK's decision to leave the consortium at the beginning of 1989. France and Italy then withdrew immediately and shortly afterwards the project collapsed completely.

The UK declared that it would pursue a national replacement for the Type 42 destroyers, the Future Frigate, and had determined that they would use the Principal Anti-Air Missile System – the same AAW system as the French and Italians. Within a year of beginning the Future Frigate, it was seen as politically expedient to cooperate with France on a new joint frigate project to carry this missile system, the Anglo-French Future Frigate. Bi-national design teams were established and work began but this, too, was short-lived. In 1992, in order to include all three governments participating in the Principal Anti-Air Missile System, the UK, France and Italy agreed to build a Common New Generation Frigate called the *Horizon* project. Although the international programmes for the development of the joint frigate and common missile system were interlinked, it was agreed that they would operate in parallel.

By 1998 the UK was prepared to commit to build 12 ships, whereas France and Italy required only 2 each rather than the similar numbers originally assumed. In this context the UK believed it was making disproportionate compromises. Despite seven years of study it became too difficult to agree a viable and equitable industrial structure for the project. In April 1999 the UK reluctantly withdrew from the *Horizon* programme (but not from the Principal Anti-Air Missile System project) and announced that it would instead develop a national design – the Type 45 destroyer. Italy and France

RIGHT Two warships derived from Common New Generation Frigate – HMS *Diamond* (foreground) and FS *Forbin* – on exercise, 2012. *(Crown Copyright, 2012 LA(Phot) Gary Weatherston)*

continued to develop a slightly smaller version of the *Horizon* frigates, each ordering two ships in October 2001. The Principal Anti-Air Missile System continued as a tripartite project with two variants; the UK version came to be called Sea Viper.

The advent of the Type 45 destroyer programme

Having decided on a national programme in 1999, the task that faced the UK's MoD and industry was to design and build the First of Class Type 45, *Daring*, to meet the planned schedule for UK ships determined by the Common New Generation Frigate programme. This timescale reflected the urgency of paying-off the last of the Type 42 destroyers with their obsolescent equipment. Because of their age these were becoming increasingly expensive to maintain as each year passed, and these costs would grow as the Type 42 destroyers came to the end of their life over the next decade. The challenge was, in a period of just over seven years, to design the warship (and a great deal of new equipment), build the ship, complete outfitting and undertake tests and trials so that *Daring* could enter service, ideally, by 2007. The programme was exceedingly ambitious and depended on the success of the highly innovative programme for Sea Viper and its associated Sampson MFR. The delivery of the Type 45 to programme would also depend on the successful and timely supply of a number of national programmes for new equipment. The most significant of these was the novel IEPS.

There was an underlying assumption that participation in the *Horizon* programme would provide a firm basis for the Type 45. However, a heavier radar, the desire to use electrical propulsion, the provision of extra space for future enhancements and the reversal of some compromises meant that very little could be salvaged from the *Horizon* work. Fortunately, the UK would be able to call upon highly experienced ship designers who had recently honed their skills on the *Horizon* programme. The two main UK companies involved in *Horizon* (GEC Marine and British Aerospace) employed many of these engineers, and GEC Marine owned significant shipbuilding facilities. Just

before the UK withdrew from *Horizon* these two companies had agreed that they would merge to form BAE Systems in November 1999.

The MoD's intention was to encourage industry to form a risk-sharing alliance, but such innovative procurement arrangements could not be negotiated rapidly. With MoD agreement, BAE Systems formed a wholly-owned subsidiary company, Type 45 Prime Contract Office, that would be offered, in the first instance, an initial contract for the design. A MoD Project Team would regularly review and guide the work on the basis of 'eyes on, hands off'. The two teams would operate together with complementary responsibilities as an Integrated Project Team. All members of the team would have access to the project management tools and would engage in regular formal reviews to monitor progress and potential barriers to achieving milestones or cost targets.

The formal start of the project (coinciding with the formation of BAE Systems in November 1999) was the award for the first phase, a one-year contract for 'Preparation for Demonstration' to the Prime Contract Office. The contract called for the Prime Contract Office to be totally responsible for the development of *Daring* (with overall design authority), for acquisition of the equipment and materials, and for contracting the ship's building and trials. Unlike aircraft, for which BAE Systems had already been a prime contractor, warships have no prototypes for evaluation before production building begins. A First of Class warship enters service and is not

ABOVE Two Type 45 destroyers, HMS *Daring* and HMS *Diamond* in Portsmouth Naval Base towering over the paid-off Batch III Type 42 destroyer HMS *Gloucester*.
(Steve Wright)

discarded like aircraft prototypes. Unfortunately, the prime contractor would not have direct control of contracts for key developmental items such as Sea Viper and the long-range radar (LRR), as international contracts had already been placed for their supply. As a consequence, neither the Prime Contract Office nor the MoD had direct control over progress of the development of this equipment.

Preparation for Demonstration contract

The contract was let with the overall requirement to meet nine Key User Requirements. During this initial phase, the Prime Contract Office was tasked with producing an outline design for the national destroyer to a level necessary to demonstrate that it was viable, and to obtain an estimate of costs for the development and manufacture of the First of Class, *Daring*. They would define the warship in more detailed engineering terms and document this in a comprehensive Contractor's System Requirements Document. An unprecedented

80% of *Daring*'s equipment would be new to service and specifically developed for the class. This meant that it was not possible to firmly specify the detailed ship's characteristics and equipment before a contract was placed. The high degree of equipment innovation and development that would be undertaken in parallel with the whole ship necessitated a more flexible approach, in which the details of the specification could evolve to accommodate the maturing definitions of the equipment.

To maintain a consistent and complete specification that met the envisaged capability for the evolving design, a requirements management tool was employed. Such an approach had previously been used to manage the interrelated complexities of a warship's combat system, but never for a whole warship. The tool enabled requirements to be allocated to specific equipment and these subsets of requirements formed an important element of the subcontracts to be let.

During this short contract the design team determined the fundamental characteristics of the design. For the new equipment it was necessary to estimate the weight, dimensions and service requirements (*eg* power, cooling, etc). The range of equipment to be accommodated included equipment that could yet be procured during the ship's life as part of an Incremental Acquisition Programme. This included existing equipment (such as the Mk41 vertical launch system) and items concurrently under development as well as an allowance for undefined future equipment. While this flexibility introduced a small cost penalty for the ships, the intent was to significantly reduce subsequent costs by avoiding difficult and expensive refits that are necessary to ensure the operational currency of all warships.

The *Horizon* programme had studied a number of propulsion options and decided to use, as the baseline, a combined diesel or gas turbine arrangement. However, the UK had been moving towards a more flexible and efficient electric propulsion solution. A detailed study of 14 possible solutions involving different combinations of gas turbines, diesel engines, electrical generators, motors and propeller types was undertaken. The IEPS showed significant benefits over all the other systems, although

THE TYPE 45 KEY USER REQUIREMENTS

1. Type 45, utilising PAAMS, shall be able to protect, with a probability of escaping hit of [*classified quantity omitted*], all units operating within 6.5km against up to eight supersonic sea-skimming missiles arriving randomly within [*classified quantity omitted*] seconds.
2. Type 45 shall be capable of providing anti-air warfare situational awareness covering 1,000 airborne objects against a departure/arrival rate of 500/hour.
3. Type 45 shall be able to provide close tactical control to at least four, fixed-wing or groups of, aircraft.
4. Type 45 shall be able to operate both one Merlin and Lynx Mk8 helicopter, although not simultaneously.
5. Type 45 shall be able to operate an embarked military force of at least 30 deployable troops.
6. Type 45 shall carry a medium-calibre gun system of at least 114mm.
7. Type 45 shall be able to travel at least 3,000 nautical miles, operate for three days and return within 20 days unsupported.
8. Type 45 shall be able to be upgraded to incorporate new capabilities or expand extant capabilities.
9. Type 45 shall have a 70% availability to contribute to operations over a period of not less than 25 years a minimum of 35% of which must be spent at sea.

this type of propulsion system was untried on a warship of this size. It was judged the best way to achieve the requirements, especially because of the reduced maintenance costs, fuel costs and whole-life costs. In order to reduce uncertainties it was decided to award an Electric Ship Technology Demonstrator (ESTD) contract to begin development immediately.

Contract for Demonstration and First-of-Class Manufacture

Until this point, it had been common for warship projects to involve a large number of contractual stages, with work slowing or stopping between contracts while the MoD reviewed the project and obtained funds for the next phase. For *Daring* there would be only two contractual phases with a seamless transition between them.

On 20 December 2000 a contract for the second phase was awarded to the Prime Contract Office. This contract, entitled Demonstration and First-of-Class Manufacture, encompassed the design, development and building of the First of Class Type 45 and two further Type 45s. The contract also included the supply of six sets of 'long lead' equipment for the manufacture of possible further ships. The delivery programme was for full acceptance of the ships (later known as *Daring*, *Dauntless* and *Diamond*) in September 2007, March 2009 and September 2009 respectively. This was broadly in line with the UK's previous programme for *Horizon* frigates.

The contract was revised on 18 February 2002 to cover the delivery of six platforms in total, with an option for a further two (that was not, in fact, invoked). In the meantime, however, detailed planning had revealed that the programme was overambitious and a delay of at least a year would be inevitable. This was accepted in the contract.

During the first two years the Prime Contract Office would flesh out the design and produce details that would allow production to begin. The technical specification was the Contractor's System Requirements Document that had been developed during the previous Preparation for

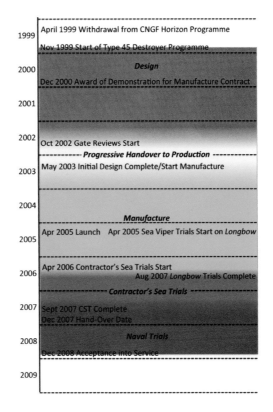

LEFT The Demonstration and First-of-Class Manufacture programme (2002). *(Author)*

Demonstration phase. Further details would be added to this specification with the rationale for decisions recorded in Design Disclosure documents produced by the design teams.

The Prime Contract Office would also be responsible for specifying and placing major contracts for equipment (usually by competition) and for negotiating and awarding contracts with shipbuilders. However, some existing equipment (the medium-calibre gun system and decoys) and development items (in particular the Sea Viper equipment) would be provided as Government-furnished equipment, as contracts for these were already in place.

Design development of *Daring*

The design of *Daring* continued seamlessly from the Preparation for Demonstration contract to the follow-on Demonstration and First-of-Class Manufacture contract.

The pace of the work then increased as the design was developed in more detail. Warship design is highly interactive, with small changes in one aspect having potentially major impacts elsewhere. Several interrelated strands of work were undertaken as related overleaf:

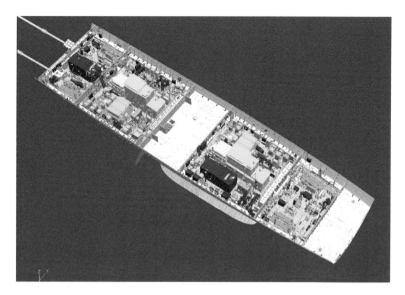

ABOVE **3D compartment model.** *(BAE Systems)*

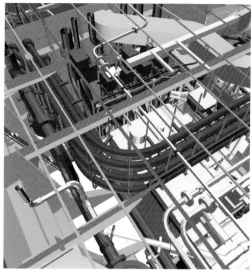

ABOVE **3D pipework model to determine routing and potential clashes.** *(BAE Systems)*

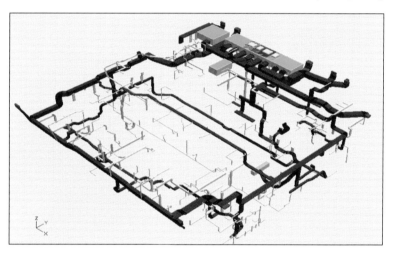

ABOVE **Cable routing model.** *(BAE Systems)*

BELOW **Structural model.** *(BAE Systems)*

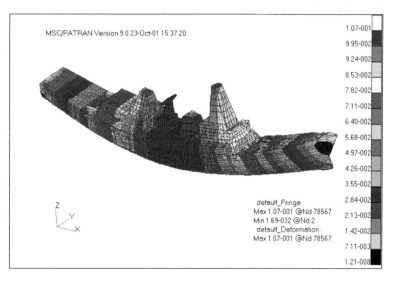

Physical design

The traditional 2D general arrangement drawings were replaced by 3D representations as the design evolved. Weight and volume estimates became more accurate as the design progressed with more detail of equipment and ship's service systems (electrical power, chilled water, etc) progressed. The 3D representations were also used to determine the routing of pipework, services and cabling. The increasing amount of data was collated using databases that would eventually become the repository of equipment data for the ship during build and the source of documents such as the Bill of Material.

The 3D description of the ship allowed detailed calculations to be performed using various computer-modelling techniques, for instance modelling structural strength that could highlight potential areas of weakness. Sea-keeping is not yet able to be fully modelled using a computer so scale models were built in a towing tank to test the hull's performance.

In previous warships, special MoD standards were applied to ensure that the ship met appropriate general requirements for warships relating to structural strength, stability and a range of factors relating to operational standards. However, for some years the MoD had been developing warship classification standards with Lloyd's Register that would not only take into account mandatory commercial

safety and environmental regulations, but also emphasise the standards relating to specific naval conditions of a warship going in harm's way. The Type 45 destroyers were the first warships to comply with specifically naval standards established by a commercial classification society.

Transverse activities

Design factors such as survivability, safety, reliability, ship's signatures and electro-magnetic compatibility must be addressed on a ship-wide basis. Designers concentrating on a single aspect of the design (such as the propulsion system or combat system)

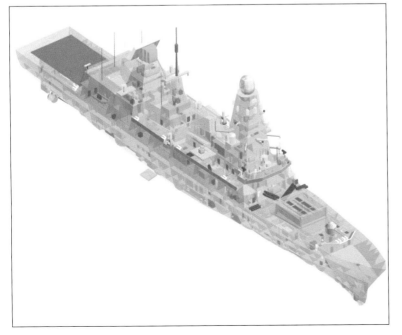

TOP Physical model undergoing sea-keeping trials. (QinetiQ)

ABOVE Haslar towing tank. (QinetiQ)

LEFT Vulnerability model. (QinetiQ)

BELOW Electromagnetic model. (Selex ES)

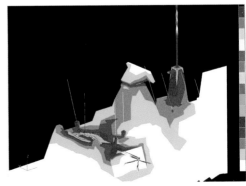

cannot work in isolation. The engineers who control transverse activities have to ensure that the impact that any one system makes is not disproportionate and that overall targets for the ship are achieved. Again, modelling was used extensively to rapidly identify any areas of difficulty, allowing the designers to concentrate on devising solutions to the most pressing problems. For instance, a survivability model (QinetiQ's SURVIVE software tool) was used to assess the susceptibility, vulnerability and recoverability of the vessel under a variety of threat weapon scenarios. Complex electro-magnetic modelling was also used to investigate the interaction between the ship's antennas and its superstructure and weather-deck equipment. The work reduces unwanted interactions and ensures that the antennas are optimally positioned on the superstructure.

Functional design

Daring relies on a number of systems that incorporate significant software, in particular the combat systems equipment and propulsion equipment. Such systems also exchange a great deal of data with other equipment, and these data flows had to be understood before the software could be written. During this period of design much effort was required to negotiate and define a set of mutually compatible data exchange specifications. These ensure that data that each type of equipment exchanges with other equipment is correct for the equipment's effective operation. Originally developed for combat systems equipment, these techniques were now not only more sophisticated but were also used to develop the propulsion and other ship's systems that were heavily dependent on software.

The ship was to have several data networks, and planning of these at an early stage ensured that sufficient capacity was provided for the exchange of data between equipment, and that the requisite physical locations had connections. It was essential, for instance, that the many communications terminals and voice users' units throughout the ship could all have data connections.

Contracting

The detailed requirements that would be necessary to meet the key user requirements were analysed and expanded using a requirements management computer tool. This enabled the accurate and consistent set of specifications to be produced for material and equipment that would be supplied by contractors. The Prime Contract Office, as part of BAE Systems, drew upon the organisation's commercial expertise. Suppliers were selected, usually after a competition, at an earlier stage than ever before on a warship programme. By mid-2002, 13 of the 14 major contracts (representing over 80% of supply by value) were in place, including two shipbuilding contracts. By the end of 2003 all were in place, as were 60 contracts with suppliers who would provide equipment and who would later support the ship design process through detailed design and construction. Over 400 other contractors were identified to supply standard equipment and catalogue material (about 10% by value). These would be placed and managed by the shipbuilders.

Project management

A detailed programme was established identifying the plethora of activities and major milestones necessary to deliver the ship. The foreseen programme risks were recorded along with the likely effects of any dislocation on the delivery timescale and cost. For major risks, mitigating strategies were devised. Throughout the initial years of the project, earned value management was used to determine the variation from the budgeted costs, indicating the potential for schedule overrun or increased costs.

With such an innovative vessel there were real possibilities that unforeseen technical problems would result in late delivery of equipment under development. It is the task of project managers to identify the impact of these problems and conceive schedule adjustments that would lessen the consequences. Technical solutions require the very best engineers and may be impossible to achieve without slippage in the programme. When this occurs the cry is often that there should have been 'more project management'. However, provided that the project management is sufficient to monitor the programme (and produce mitigating strategies), additional project management cannot overcome severe technical difficulties. Solutions to such difficulties require experienced engineers.

Build strategy

The Prime Contract Office was responsible for awarding and managing the shipbuilding activities due to begin in 2003. The MoD was intending to direct the Prime Contract Office to award the build of the first and third Type 45 hulls to BAE Systems and the second hull to VT Group, these shipbuilders being the only ones in the UK capable of undertaking the work. Potential extensions to the contracts for three further hulls were to be the subject of competitive tendering. The shipyard with the lower price would build two hulls and the other offered the third at the same price.

However, the Prime Contract Office proposed an alternative strategy – a whole-programme, shared-build arrangement whereby each of the shipyards would build sections of the ship. BAE Systems's two yards and VT Group's yard in Portsmouth would each fabricate specific parts that would then be assembled as hulls in a single shipyard. This strategy would allow VT Group to move from Southampton to occupy valuable but under-exploited facilities in Portsmouth Naval Base, where they would fabricate the bow section, mast structures and funnel.

The commercial stability afforded by this arrangement allowed both companies to invest in advanced production facilities such as covered halls, new slipways, improved dry-dock facilities, automated machinery and a load-out quay. The cost of the new facilities in Portsmouth was £50 million, and those associated with the dry dock in Scotstoun were £20 million. Although this dual-location strategy would involve the non-recurring cost of acquiring a transport barge and costs of each transfer, it was anticipated that efficiency savings would more than outweigh these costs. Apart from acquiring a trained workforce and modern facilities for the future, the strategy secured the potential for future competition. BAE Systems acquired VT Group's shipbuilding facilities in October 2009, the two companies having previously placed their shipbuilding activities in a joint venture company for about 15 months, thereby combining all the build facilities for the Type 45 destroyers in a single organisation.

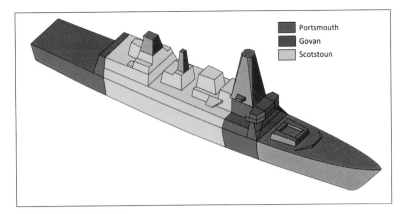

Portsmouth
Govan
Scotstoun

Long-term strategy

During the first years of the contract it was essential to map out strategies for the trials programme, the acceptance of the First of Class and for the training and support of the class of warships when in service.

Transition from development to production

During the design development a number of Design Reviews were held involving customer representatives. The reviews ensured that the design intent was consistent and ensured that the customer had visibility of design decisions. Even though information from suppliers of some development equipment was still tentative, from the beginning of 2002 the shipyards were asked to develop detailed production drawings of certain compartments once they had been subjected to a Gate Review. From mid-2003 the design was 'frozen', after which any change was subject not only to tight configuration control but also to intense scrutiny to ensure that all ramifications of the change were covered by modifications to drawings. From this time the design was released progressively to the shipyards to complete detailed 3D design and production drawings.

In early 2003, BAE Systems decided that it would reorganise its naval business. As a consequence, the Prime Contract Office was absorbed into the shipbuilding organisation and lost its independent control of the programme. There were significant and premature losses of experienced staff as they moved to new projects or were made redundant in the reorganisation. As a consequence, the effective and close working relationship with the MoD disappeared. In previous designs the MoD had controlled the development and then passed the design to a shipbuilder to prepare production drawings. The compromises and rationale behind design decisions were not always understood, even where these were carefully documented. It was found that this lack of continuity could result in previous decisions being overturned because the disadvantages seemed more evident than the justification and beneficial concessions of those decisions. One of the reasons for having the Prime Contract Office had been to ensure continuity during the transition to the build phase and see that the integrity of the design intent was maintained. Unfortunately, the reorganisation within BAE Systems for unrelated commercial reasons resulted in a turbulent transition.

During 2003 there was debate both within the MoD and BAE Systems about the meaning of prime contracting and the extent to which industry could be a design authority without the MoD abrogating its duty-holder responsibilities. It was clear that, in this instance, only the MoD could manage the major risks associated with the Sea Viper and other associated programmes that would be supplied as Government-furnished equipment.

The shipbuilder could only be called the prime contractor in the sense that it was responsible for the construction and for sub-contracting the functional integration of the systems. Its only risk related to aspects not affected by any Government-furnished equipment or information. Although BAE Systems was nominally still the Design Authority, and liable for producing a Certificate of Design, much of the accountability reverted to the MoD duty-holders.

To complicate matters further, there was an extreme shortage of computer-aided design operators because of delays to other BAE Systems naval programmes and external demands from several large civil engineering projects. This further slowed progress on the detailed design. For this and other reasons, the shipbuilder negotiated a further delay to the programme in 2004, with a Contractor's Acceptance Date of May 2009.

Production

The first steel for the Type 45 destroyer programme was cut on 28 March 2003, for a prototype foremast. This mast would eventually be used for trials of the Sampson MFR and would not be used for building a ship. The first steel to be cut for the main build was on 11 August 2003.

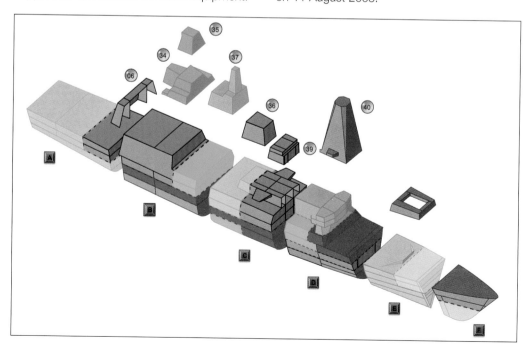

RIGHT **Type 45 hull blocks and units.** *(Author from BAE Systems information)*

Daring was built in blocks in three different yards. The blocks were then transported by barge to Scotstoun on the River Clyde for assembly into a single hull before launch. BAE Systems fabricated most of *Daring* on Clydeside – Blocks A (the stern) and D in their Govan facility and Blocks B and C in their Scotstoun yard. The machinery blocks, B and C, form the centre section of the ship. Before they were joined to the other blocks they were fitted with their large items of propulsion equipment such as GTAs, diesel alternators and propulsion motors. Meanwhile, a single bow section (Blocks E/F) and other items were manufactured in Portsmouth.

During fabrication, the blocks were pre-outfitted with 11,500 sections of pipe and ducting. The open canoe technique was used, where units of the blocks were built and equipment installed without the deckhead in place. Meanwhile, the deckhead was fabricated upside down so that pipes and ducting could be installed using down-hand welding wherever possible. The deckhead was then turned shipwise and welded into place to complete the unit. Over 2,400 items of equipment were installed before launch, including the 90-tonne gas turbine module and other propulsion equipment mentioned earlier. Standardisation of parts was used to reduce the number of types and standards of plate thickness, couplings and brackets. This not only provides economies of scale but also reduces the Bill of Materials and the number of installation standards. It yields production efficiencies and also reduces support costs by minimising the stores holdings and by improving the ability to interchange parts of the ship.

In total 2,800 tonnes of steel were used to build *Daring*'s hull – enough to build Blackpool tower. The masts were the only major items not incorporated before *Daring* was launched. The area of the steelwork used in the hull was about 100,000m^2 (more than four times the area of Trafalgar Square). Traditionally solvent-based paint has been used to protect warships, but the Type 45 destroyers are protected by a powder-coating process. Where this innovative process could not be used, water-based paint was substituted, or, for the weather decks, hard-wearing non-slip epoxy coatings. All these coatings meet current, stringent environmental standards.

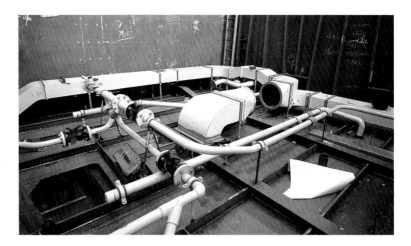

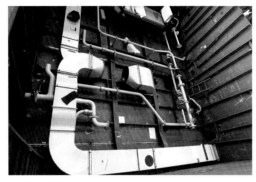

ABOVE AND LEFT
Downhand installation of pipes and trunking prior to final assembly of unit. *(BAE Systems)*

ABOVE Type 45 bow section (Blocks E/F), masts and other units transported by barge from Portsmouth to the River Clyde. *(John Crae)*

LEFT Type 45 bow section being prepared for offloading from barge. *(Stuart Cameron)*

Block A, the 700-tonne stern unit, was successfully transported from Govan to the Scotstoun yard in December 2004. There it was moved to its final launch position on the berth in preparation for link-up with the other sections of the ship.

Self-propelled modular trailers were used to move the blocks arriving from Portsmouth and Govan from their barges, and to transport them to the slipway from which the completed hull would eventually be launched. The carrier can accurately align the block over the slipway.

Once in its correct position over the slipway, the weight of the block was then transferred to the cylindrical hydraulic jacks of a synchronous lifting system. Once the block was fully supported by the hydraulic jacks the multi-wheeled carrier was removed. The hydraulic pressure in the jacks measured the actual weight and centre of gravity of the block, allowing *Daring*'s design calculations to be confirmed for the first time. Two side tracks, running down either side of the slipway, were laid. These would support the weight of the blocks as they were joined to form the hull. The hydraulic jacks then lowered the block synchronously so that its weight was evenly transferred to the side tracks.

Each block arriving at the slipway ('incoming block') had 50mm excess steel ('green' margin) where it was to be welded to its adjacent block. The blocks were slid together on the slipway and three-point measurements were taken to validate precision of fit. The incoming block was screeved, the excess metal removed, the block moved hard against its adjacent block and the two welded together using a trolley-mounted KAT oscillator. The blocks were successively joined on the slipway to form the hull. Finally, Block D from Govan and Blocks E/F from Portsmouth were delivered in June 2005 and joined together that October. As the blocks were joined, the pre-outfitting of compartments and installation of the fluid systems were completed ahead of reeving 150km of cabling. The consolidation of the blocks into a single 5,222-tonne hull was completed by November 2005.

ABOVE *Dauntless* stern section (Block A) being transported to the slipway and aligned on multi-wheeled carrier. *(Enerpac BV)*

RIGHT A block being lowered by the cylindrical hydraulic jacks of the synchronous lifting system and the load transferred on to the side tracks. *(Enerpac BV)*

LEFT Slipway preparation for *Daring* launch. *(Stuart Cameron)*

The connection of pipes and cables between blocks and further pre-outfitting were undertaken with *Daring* on the slipway prior to launch, including the fitting of the 94 modular accommodation cabins. Modular standardisation of the cabin build reduced the costs of manufacture and installation (with installation time reduced to about 25% of that required to build bespoke cabins). The majority were delivered as sealed, fully equipped and inspected assemblies ready for installation. However, 26 were 'flat packs' for those positions where limited access demanded that they were assembled within the blocks.

Ship launch

On Wednesday 1 February 2006, half an hour before high water (when the river is at greatest depth), *Daring* was ready for launch. She was sitting on a slipway comprising two pairs of wooden platforms called a sliding way and a standing way, and restrained by four large catches called triggers. Without these triggers the force of gravity would cause the sliding way to move over the top of the standing way. The lady sponsor, HRH the Countess of Wessex, broke a bottle of champagne on the bow and formally named the ship *Daring*.

When the bottle broke, BAE Systems's harbour master pushed a button to release the triggers and *Daring* accelerated to 5m/sec as she slid into the Clyde. The electronic mechanism that released the triggers had been carefully designed, but in the unlikely event of it failing to release the ship there was the fallback of using a traditional launch method – four men with sledgehammers to knock out the triggers manually! Having reached the river, the ship's progress was slowed by 680 tonnes of drag-chains attached to the ship. The drag-chains were 40 tonnes heavier on the port side so that as *Daring* slowed she also turned downriver.

Outfitting

Following launch, *Daring* moved the short distance to Elderslie dry dock to complete construction and outfitting. To prepare the dock for a ship as large and complex as *Daring* an investment was made in refurbishing the

ABOVE *Daring* being prepared for launch. *(BAE Systems)*

LEFT *Daring* launched from the Scotstoun Yard. *(Crown Copyright, 2006 FRPU(N))*

BELOW Aerial view of the launch of *Daring*. *(Crown Copyright, 2006 FRPU(N))*

RIGHT Aerial view of *Daring* undergoing outfitting in dry dock. *(Crown Copyright, 2007 LA(Phot) Massey)*

dock facilities. These changes included a new sonar pit, an extension to an existing pit, a new hauling-in system, modifications to the dock gate and the assembly of new modular accommodation and facilities buildings adjacent to the dry dock.

Because of a height restriction, *Daring* was launched without its foremast, which was added once the ship was in dry dock. Later the extremely challenging task of installing the Sampson Multifunction Radar (MFR) on to the foremast would be undertaken. This radar, weighing over seven tonnes, would be successfully lifted more than 40m in the air from the side of the dry dock (by a crane capable of stretching halfway across the dry dock) and lowered on to the bearing ring at the top of the foremast. There is only a small clearance between the equipment that hangs beneath the radar and the bearing ring through which it has to pass. As a consequence, the radar has to be lowered with extreme precision.

The LRR presented different challenges. Its mast was delivered as a module that contained all of its equipment pre-installed. Once this was welded to the superstructure, the radar antenna was lifted into position and installed. Other major items that had to be lifted on to the ship during outfitting were the medium-calibre gun (MCG) and the six Sylver launcher modules.

A number of commercial off-the-shelf techniques were employed during the manufacturing process to speed outfitting and reduce hot work. These techniques included standard struts that were welded into place before launch. During outfitting equipment was bolted to these struts in order to avoid further welding. In addition, pipes were joined using sleeve couplings that also avoided welding.

RIGHT Installing the foremast. *(BAE Systems)*

FAR LEFT Installing
Sampson multifunction
radar. *(BAE Systems)*

LEFT Installing the
Long Range Radar
antenna. *(BAE Systems)*

Daring has several data highways interconnecting more than 700 circuits using fibre optic networks often employing complex routes. A typical route is shorter than 100m but passes through a dozen decks or bulkheads, requires a similar number of right-angled bends and needs up to eight fibre optic cables to transmit the data. The technology adopted was blown optical fibre. Although commonly used for long-distance communication along almost straight routes, this technique had not been used previously for warship applications. Major trials of the technology were undertaken before the technique was adopted. Investigations included determining the type of standard cable seal that could be used where the networks

FAR LEFT Installing
the medium-calibre
gun. *(BAE Systems)*

LEFT Installing a
Sylver eight-missile
launcher module.
(BAE Systems)

penetrated decks or bulkheads. These penetrations, employed throughout the ship, need to form a watertight seal, a fire barrier or both. Blown optical fibre involved the installation of a network of hollow micro-ducts throughout the ship. As the ship neared completion, several optical fibres were blown through each of these micro-ducts by compressed air. Not only did the data networks prove quick to install, but the technology also permitted simple and rapid alteration to fibre optic cable configurations without major disruption, thereby providing adequate scope for future upgrades.

About 20,000 electrical power cables with a total length of over 600km were installed – enough to circle the M25 more than three times. On previous ships cable and data penetrations were welded in place. On the Type 45 new watertight and fireproof 'Rubber Insert Sleeve (Expanding)' cable penetrations were adopted, as they were faster to install and required no hot work. The insert sleeve expands with the application of heat, thereby forming a fire barrier. The penetrations are also more appropriate for carrying a mixture of power cables and data highway micro-ducts through the same aperture. For instance, the flexible rubber reduces cable stress and provides some noise isolation.

Development of the integrated electric propulsion system (IEPS)

The Type 45 destroyer's IEPS was designed to provide the means to propel the ship while simultaneously powering all electrically-driven equipment. In essence, it is a small seagoing power station capable of producing enough electricity to supply a city the size of Dundee. The power is supplied by two GTAs supplemented by two diesel alternators. The propulsion system has a twin-shaft configuration, with each propeller shaft driven by an electric advanced induction motor (AIM).

For many years, the main source of propulsive power on RN warships has been provided by gas turbines. Large and heavy gearboxes are required to match the speed of rotation of the turbines to that needed to rotate the propellers. However, the desired endurance requirements and the need to reduce running costs required a new, more efficient arrangement for the Type 45 destroyers. A major challenge of the IEPS development was to provide sufficient power within the physical constraints imposed by the hull of a warship. This high power-density was realised by adopting advanced air-cooling for the two propulsion motors that would turn the propellers without a gearbox. These AIMs were developed from standard 3-phase, 15-channel industrial induction motors. The AIMs have a larger air gap between the stator and rotor in order to meet naval standards for withstanding the shock of underwater explosions. The pulse-width modulated control, waveform type and multiphase design mean that the motors exhibit low noise signatures and reduced harmonic field current.

Two gas turbine prime movers were evaluated for the Type 45 – the simple-cycle GE LM2500 gas turbine and the Rolls-Royce WR-21 marine gas turbine. The WR-21 was the only advanced-cycle marine gas turbine available and the first production aero-derivative plant to incorporate both compressor intercooling and exhaust heat recuperation technologies – technologies that deliver low specific fuel consumption across the engine's entire operating range. The choice was between the attractively priced LM2500, and the new WR-21 that was more complex and higher priced but more economical to operate. In addition to providing lower and more uniform fuel consumption at either high or low power, a further advantage of the WR-21 is that the intercooled and recuperated units recycle energy from the hot exhaust gases, reducing the warship's infrared signature. The two machines have similar footprints, but the WR-21's intercooled and recuperated equipment means that it is more than one deck higher, about 25% bulkier and 125% heavier than the LM2500 marine gas turbine.

A reduction of the 'through life cost' of operation and maintenance has been a desire for a number of years, yet it is often sacrificed to the expedience of reduced initial acquisition costs (unit production cost). In this case, however, the danger of rising fuel costs over the life of the class and the need to reduce maintenance prevailed and the WR-21 was selected.

By the beginning of the Type 45 destroyer project in 1999, the WR-21 had just completed testing at the former National Gas Turbine Establishment. The tests involved the WR-21 providing power through a gearbox to two static dynamometers. While this showed that the advanced cycle gas turbine met all the desired performance characteristics, it still had to be proven as part of the overall IEPS, an arrangement that would first be demonstrated on *Daring*. To develop the IEPS the MoD had commissioned, in a joint Anglo-French programme, the ESTD test site as a means of investigating and proving the high-power electric propulsion systems of *Daring* and future ships such as the HMS *Queen Elizabeth* aircraft carriers. This demonstrator would bring together for the first time the WR-21, the alternator that it would drive, the AIM and other components of the electrical propulsion system such as the converters. This would allow the propulsion system to be established independently of *Daring*. Tests that could not wait to be conducted on *Daring* (or that required equipment that would not be on board *Daring*) could be carried out separately from the warship development and build.

Because the IEPS was unproven, the ESTD provided a means of reducing its technical risk and uncertainty for *Daring*, particularly any system integration issues. Importantly, it demonstrated the performance of the complete propulsion system rather than just the stand-alone performance of individual equipment. Further, it allowed the exploration of the system's electro-magnetic compatibility and validation of mathematical software models. Such models of the equipment and of the system reduce the need for extensive shore testing and assist with later ship designs. The ESTD is a full-scale arrangement of actual propulsion equipment that allows detailed investigation of the potential and boundaries of this marine engineering technology. Long after the entry into service of the destroyer's propulsion system, it continues to influence the development of propulsion systems for international warship programmes.

Construction of the ESTD began in 2001 and was completed two years later. Initial testing concentrated on the 21MWe 4.16kV WR-21 GTA set, followed by an intense period of commissioning in preparation for Phase 1 trials. Initially the facility had two additional power sources: a 4MWe 4.16kV Typhoon GTA and 1MWe 440V diesel alternator. A 12MVA 4.16kV 50Hz supply was also available through a transformer from the 11kV grid. The facility also had two items of equipment from the propulsion system, a VDM25000 converter and a 20MW AIM. The converter generates the correct waveforms to drive the AIM. Attached to this motor's flange was a novel and important piece of test equipment, the four-quadrant load. This provided an electrical load to the motor output for all current and voltage situations, whether positive or negative, to simulate the mechanical load of a propeller to its maximum (20MW) extent. The testing could thus replicate

BELOW Electric ship technology demonstrator showing the advanced induction motor and the four-quadrant load generator. *(GE Energy)*

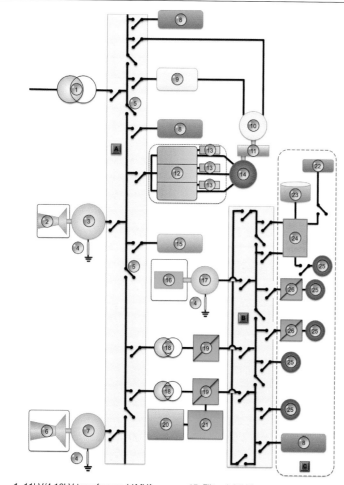

1 11kV/4.16kV transformer 11MVA 50Hz.
2 Typhoon gas turbine.
3 Alternator 4MWe 4.16V AC.
4 Neutral earthing resistors.
5 Busbar tie.
6 WR-21 gas turbine.
7 Alternator 21MWe.
8 Loadbank 4.16V A 23 MVA.
9 Four-quadrant load converter.
10 Four-quadrant load machine.
11 Gearbox.
12 VDM25000 three-channel 15ø converter.
13 Dynamic breaking resistors.
14 Advanced induction motor.

15 Filter 4.16kV.
16 Diesel engine.
17 Alternator 1 MWe 440V AC.
18 4.16kV/440V transformer.
19 Converter AC to AC or DC.
20 Bulk energy storage simulator.
21 Bulk energy storage converter.
22 Load.
23 Flywheel.
24 Zonal power supply unit.
25 Motor.
26 Converter AC to AC.

A 4.16kV switchboard.
B 440V AC or 800V DC switchboard.
C 440V loads.

LEFT Electric ship technology demonstrator single line diagram. *(Author from GE Energy information)*

all conditions experienced by the AIM when powering a propeller at sea.

In addition to the 4.16kV (medium voltage) equipment, the facility also had 440V (low voltage) equipment comprising 2MW of 440V loads, both spinning (motors) and static. To fully test the system, loads that produced harmonic distortion were included. The major load on this system was a dual-input 300kW zonal power supply unit providing multiple outputs at different voltages and frequencies in order to accurately simulate all of the warship's individual 440V loads. The zonal power supply unit stored energy in mechanical form in a 200kW flywheel, providing a high-power backup in the event of a loss of the 440V supply.

Phase 1 testing at the facility began with full-power testing of the engines. The propulsion motors, the ship services link converters and energy stores were subjected to a comprehensive set of trials. These culminated in 'seven scenarios' – a set of arduous events. These covered the most onerous tests of a marine electrical power system ever performed, including full 4.16kV and 440V short circuits, crash reversals, full-load tripping events and synchronisation of alternators out of phase. The tests included back-to-back testing of two AIMs. In these trials the shafts of two motors were physically connected so that the port motor rotated the starboard motor. The starboard motor then acted as an AC generator whose converter took the waveforms that it produces to generate direct current. By interconnecting the two converters the energy produced could be used to feed the port motor. Power thus circulated between the motors, the AC supply merely compensating for system losses.

More detailed investigations were performed during Phase 2 testing, including tests to measure the equipment's efficiency and noise characteristics as well as studies of electro-magnetic compatibility. ESTD trials were successfully concluded in October 2005. In many

LEFT Back-to-back testing of advanced induction motors. *(GE Energy)*

RIGHT Single line diagram of back-to-back testing configuration. *(Author from GE Energy information)*

cases the equipment significantly exceeded expectations. Validated models were delivered and a vast amount of data automatically recorded by the system for future analysis.

In parallel with Phase 2 trials, the site was modified to include shore integration testing of the Type 45 destroyer IEPS. For these tests, ship's equipment including 4.16kV and 440V harmonic filters, a ship's services transformer and a 2MW diesel alternator set were added to create one of the two identical power systems to be supplied to *Daring*. The tests investigated the harmonic filter operation, the quality of both the 4.16kV and 440V supplies and the operation of the GTA and diesel alternator when generating in parallel. Sufficient knowledge was gained to allow the large items of propulsion equipment to be installed on *Daring* before launch.

Once *Daring*'s power and propulsion systems were successfully set to work, full-power trials were completed while she was secured alongside the harbour wall. Such a trial had never been performed before because it had been impossible to restrain a warship, as the thrust transmitted to the propellers would tear the ship from its moorings. However, by replacing the adjustable bolted propeller blades

RIGHT Type 45 Shore Integration Test Facility single line diagram. *(Author from GE Energy information)*

BELOW Brake blades fitted for alongside full-power propulsion trial. *(GE Energy)*

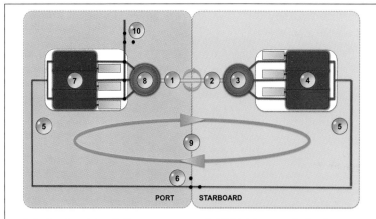

1 Port motor rotates shaft.
2 Shaft passes power to starboard motor.
3 Starboard motor generates 4.16kV AC.
4 Starboard converter changes AC to DC.
5 DC link interconnector.
6 DC link interconnector breaker.
7 Port converter changes DC to 4.16kV AC.
8 AC drives port motor.
9 Power circulation around system.
10 AC supply counteracts system losses.

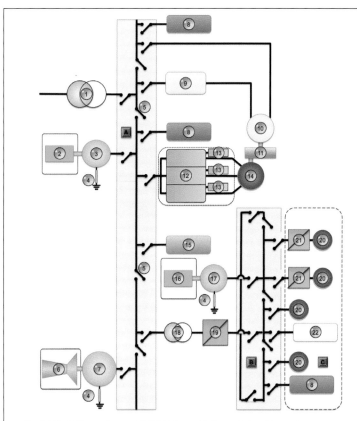

1 11kV/4.16kV transformer 11MVA 50Hz.
2 Typhoon gas turbine.
3 Alternator 4MWe 4.16V AC.
4 Neutral earthing resistors.
5 Busbar tie.
6 WR-21 gas turbine.
7 Alternator 21MWe.
8 Loadbank 4.16V A 23 MVA.
9 Four-quadrant load converter.
10 Four-quadrant load machine.
11 Gearbox.
12 VDM25000 three-channel 15ø converter.
13 Dynamic breaking resistors.
14 Advanced induction motor.
15 Filter 4.16kV.
16 Diesel engine.
17 Alternator 1MWe 440V AC.
18 4.16kV/440V transformer.
19 Converter AC to AC or DC.
20 Motor.
21 Converter AC to AC.
22 Filter 440V.
A 4.16kV switchboard.
B 440V AC or 800V DC switchboard.
C 440V loads.

RIGHT Factory
version 3. *(Author
from BAE Systems
information)*

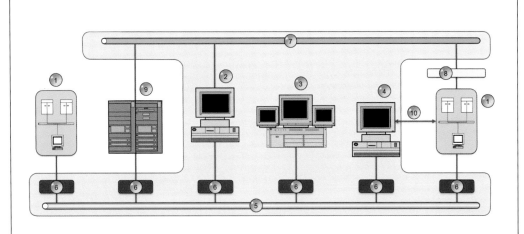

1 Combat system equipment under test.
2 Scenario generator and scenario animator.
3 Mini combat management system.
4 Software and integration test tool.
5 Data transfer system test environment.

6 Coupler.
7 High-level architecture scenario highway.
8 Simulator.
9 Combat system equipment emulator.
10 Point to point hardwired link.

with specially designed brake blades it was possible to undertake such trials even with a warship of *Daring*'s power. The blades were designed to absorb full propulsive power while developing very little thrust. Divers could replace the brake blades with normal blades within a few hours, thereby allowing the ship to proceed to sea trials without the need for further expensive and time-consuming dry-docking.

Development of the combat system

The combat system includes several major new sub-systems that were specifically developed for the Type 45. These sub-systems are highly interdependent and software-intensive. A major challenge was to ensure that their software was developed in an integrated and consistent manner. This was achieved using a number of test facilities incorporating prototype hardware and software.

The key sub-system, the combat management system (CMS), was developed using a combat system Preliminary Integration Facility. Parts of this facility formed a series of Factory Support Environments that were supplied to developers of other combat system equipment. These environments included communication equipment, data transfer system (DTS) and Sampson MFR processing software that helped test the interfaces and interactions between their equipment and the rest of the combat system.

The Factory Support Environment used prototype versions of CMS software and hardware. Over time three versions were produced, with each more sophisticated than the version that it replaced. The third and final version comprised a scenario generator, a miniature version of the CMS, a software and integration trials tool and DTS. This was also used as the DTS test environment to ensure that the DTS functioned correctly when operating at maximum capacity. Equipment developers tested their equipment by

RIGHT Maritime
Integration and
Support Centre.
(Chris Gunns)

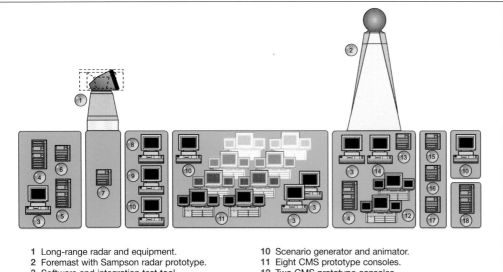

1 Long-range radar and equipment.
2 Foremast with Sampson radar prototype.
3 Software and integration test tool.
4 Combat management system server.
5 Data transfer systems equipment.
6 Precise time and frequency equipment.
7 Trials recording and integration equipment.
8 Navigation system.
9 Meteorological and oceanographic equipment.

10 Scenario generator and animator.
11 Eight CMS prototype consoles.
12 Two CMS prototype consoles.
13 Sylver launcher simulator.
14 Sampson radar integration tool.
15 Electro-optical gun control system processor.
16 Medium-calibre gun simulator.
17 Small-calibre gun simulator.
18 Medium frequency sonar processor.

LEFT Schematic of Maritime Integration and Support Centre showing typical arrangement during initial combat system integration. *(Author from BAE Systems information)*

connecting to the Factory Support Environment and an emulator that represented the software responses of other combat system equipment. Where necessary, simulators supplied inputs to the equipment under test. Testing of radar processing software, for instance, required the input of realistic radar tracks.

Traditionally the combat system is first brought together on the First of Class. However, as combat systems increase in complexity and in the amount of software that they use, this process has taken more time. In order to decouple the integration of the combat system from the ship programme, a new approach was taken. This was to build a Maritime Integration and Support Centre that would bring together prototype equipment for development and, as equipment hardware was released, actual equipment hardware. The combat system could thus be fully tested before its installation on real ships. The facility would always have the latest software releases and contribute to its final development. The use of such an external facility enabled any problems to be discovered and resolved early in the ship's programme.

The Maritime Integration and Support Centre was supplied with a foremast and LRR mast identical to those on the destroyers, as well as a prototype Sampson MFR and an operational LRR. The building reflects the profile of the

destroyer. This ensured that any performance issues or interference problems relating to external equipment could be identified and addressed early in the ship's production.

Development of Sea Viper (Guided Weapon System 45)

The Sea Viper AAW system is the Type 45 destroyer's main armament. It was the UK variant of the Principal Anti-Air Missile System developed by a tri-national team alongside a Franco-Italian variant. The two variants began with many elements in common but there were

BELOW HMS *Daring* in her home port of Portsmouth, with the Maritime Integration and Support Centre in the background. *(Chris Gunns)*

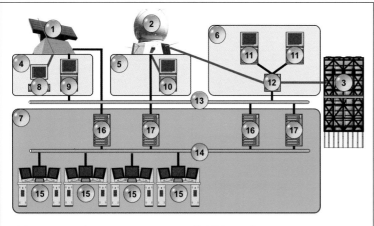

1 Long-range radar.
2 Sampson multifunction radar.
3 Sylver launcher.
4 LRR equipment room.
5 MFR equipment room.
6 Sea Viper equipment room.
7 Operations complex.
8 LRR maintenance facility.
9 LRR console.

10 MFR console.
11 C² console.
12 C² main processor unit.
13 Data transfer system.
14 CMS-1 local area network.
15 CMS-1 console.
16 CMS-1 server No 1.
17 CMS-1 server No 2.

ABOVE Sea Viper
original command and
control architecture.
*(Author from BAE
Systems information)*

BELOW Sea Viper
revised command and
control architecture.
*(Author from BAE
Systems information)*

major differences. For instance, the Sampson
MFR was being developed solely for Sea
Viper. Both systems used Aster-15 and Aster-
30 missiles, although there was a challenge
to ensure that both variants could exchange
data with the missiles. The Aster-15 missile
development was already well under way and
about to enter service with the French Navy at
the beginning of the development of *Daring*.

Given the complex and interdependent
interface between the Type 45 combat

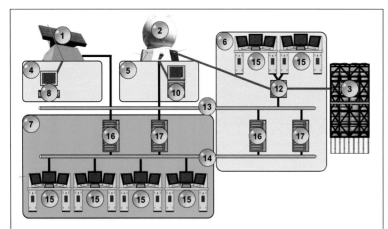

1 Long-range radar.
2 Sampson multifunction radar.
3 Sylver launcher.
4 LRR equipment room.
5 MFR equipment room.
6 Sea Viper equipment room.
7 Operations complex.
8 LRR maintenance facility.
9 (Deleted in new configuration.)

10 MFR console.
11 (Deleted in new configuration.)
12 C² main processor unit.
13 Data transfer system.
14 CMS-1 local area network.
15 CMS-1 console.
16 CMS-1 server No 1.
17 CMS-1 server No 2.

system and Sea Viper a great deal of effort
was expended in agreeing acceptable data
exchange specifications and ensuring they
met, singly and jointly, their performance
requirements. There were particular difficulties
in aligning the Sea Viper equipment programme
– determined before the Type 45 programme
started – with the extremely tight timescale of
the Type 45 programme.

In essence, the original intention was to have
two interconnected architectures. In normal
operation – about 90% of operational time –
Sea Viper would be controlled from the ship's
Operations Room as part of the integrated
combat system that provides the means of
fighting the ship in all its roles. In the event of
failure or action damage that prevented such
operation, Sea Viper could be locally controlled
from the Sea Viper Equipment Room near the
Sylver launchers. This was to be equipped
with command and control consoles from the
Franco-Italian Principal Anti-Air Missile System,
fitted to their *Horizon* frigates. In an emergency
RN operators would be using unfamiliar
consoles. This arrangement would require the
development of an additional software interface
system between the Franco-Italian consoles
and the Sampson MFR and CMS, neither of
which are fitted to *Horizon* frigates.

In complex negotiations with the Sea Viper
project and their subcontractors, the Prime
Contract Office agreed a revised architecture
that was operationally more satisfactory and of
benefit to the suppliers. The revised architecture
replaced the *Horizon* consoles with additional
CMS consoles. A pair of fallback CMS servers
were also moved from the Operations Complex
to the Sea Viper Equipment Room. There was
no longer the need to develop the complicated
software that managed the complex transition
to the emergency arrangements, thereby
significantly reducing the parallel development
demanded by more than one configuration. It
also reduced the functional load on the Sea
Viper main processor unit, as it no longer had
to process handover functions or to take on any
CMS functions.

There was now only one, integrated
configuration – but two positions from which
Sea Viper could be operated using various
combinations of identical equipment. The use

FAR LEFT Original
Sylver vertical launch
system configuration
as adopted in the
Franco-Italian frigates.
(Author)

LEFT Modified Sea
Viper Sylver vertical
launch system
configuration. *(Author)*

of the common CMS console for both positions
presents common human-computer interface
that has the advantage of reducing the time
necessary for training Sea Viper operators and
minimises confusion in the heat of battle. It
also reduced development effort and on-board
spares holdings and simplified maintenance.

A further change to the *Horizon*
arrangements was to reconfigure the Sylver
launchers from three pairs running athwartships
to two sets of three running fore and aft.
Taking into account the access requirements
of the launchers this is a more space-efficient
arrangement and gave a greater contingency if
the size of the launchers increased during their
development. It also improved ship strength by
allowing additional longitudinal structure to
be employed.

Sea Viper trials

As with all complex systems, Sea Viper
trials began with exhaustive testing of
individual elements; only when these had been
satisfactorily achieved could they be brought
together to demonstrate a complete system.

The complex and powerful Sampson MFR,
unique to Sea Viper, underwent a series
of trials designed to progressively test the
radar's performance in increasingly realistic
circumstances. In total, three prototypes

RIGHT Tests and trials of prototype Sampson
multifunction radar antennas:
(A) at the contractor's development facility;
(B) on the sea trials platform *Longbow*;
(C) at the Maritime Integration and Support
Facility *(Author)*

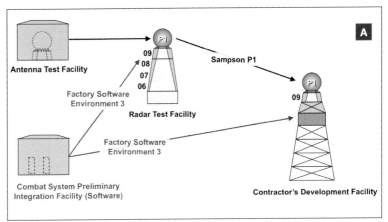

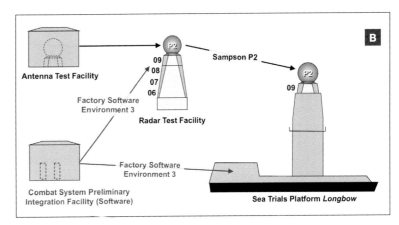

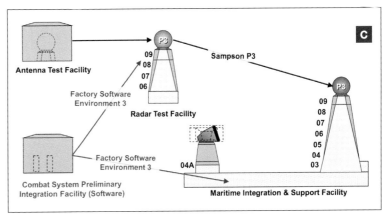

(termed P1, P2 and P3) were built and subjected to trials. After manufacture, all Sampson MFRs underwent testing in an antenna test facility at the manufacturer's site. This facility is a large hangar-like building that allows measurements to be made in highly controlled conditions. It is lined with radar-absorbent material so that the radar's own beams are not reflected from the walls, producing unwanted interference.

In Portsmouth a replica of the top four decks of the destroyer's foremast was the first item to be fabricated in the ship construction programme. This prototype was used to demonstrate the manufacturing techniques and to test the process for loading the destroyers' masts on to the seagoing barge that would be used to transport the production masts to the assembly yard in Scotland. It was moved by sea the short distance to the Isle of Wight, off-loaded and moved by road to the radar factory. There it was erected

and a Sampson MFR prototype P1 mounted on it to prove the physical interface between the mast and radar. For the first time the performance of a Sampson MFR on a mast could be investigated. Shortly afterwards a second replica mast was installed on the same site for trials of P2. A typical radar trial measured the energy at the position of the radar electronic support measures (RESM) equipment antenna beneath a Sampson MFR. Designed to detect emissions from any radar illuminating the ship, these antenna are extremely sensitive, so there was a concern that the powerful emissions of the nearby Sampson MFR would cause unacceptable interference. Such effects are extremely difficulty to predict accurately, so mitigation techniques had been developed but, in fact, proved unnecessary. Further test and qualification activities were also performed on the representative mast.

In addition to the trials masts, the Sampson MFR trials required software that represented that of the remainder of the combat system. From the beginning of the project software was being developed for both the Sea Viper systems and the remainder of the combat system. Factory Support Environments provided data representative of the inputs and responses of the rest of the combat system throughout the trials.

Prototypes P1 and P2 completed Factory Acceptance Tests in June 2006 and July 2006 respectively. P1 then moved to the Contractor's Development Facility at the Eskmeals gunnery range on the coast in Cumbria. It was again mounted on a representative mast but now raised to a height that corresponded to the height of the Sampson MFR on Type 45 destroyers. For several months from January

2007 the radar was subjected to exercises that represented increasingly realistic air attacks over sea and land.

P2 was installed on the trials barge *Longbow* in preparation for systems testing of Sea Viper. The final prototype, P3, was installed on a complete Type 45 mast at the Maritime Integration and Support Centre for integration and testing as part of a representative combat system.

While the Sampson MFR was being developed and tested on land sites, work was under way to prepare for sea trials. During 2001, BMT Defence Services Ltd carried out an extensive survey and remedial preservation of the 12,000-tonne guided weapon trials barge *Longbow* that was to serve as a sea trials platform for Sea Viper. They also undertook the design work necessary to fit a representative Sea Viper outfit, including a Sampson MFR, eight-cell Sylver A50 module and all the necessary trials equipment. *Longbow* was fitted with a 26m mast designed to support a Sampson MFR at an elevation 34m above the waterline that is representative of that on the destroyers.

BMT later assumed responsibility for the management and operation of *Longbow*, overseeing the repair, conversion and commissioning of the barge itself as well as the subsequent installation and commissioning of specific Sea Viper equipment. These systems, fitted with the latest issue of software, were integral to the *Longbow* trials programme. The refurbishment was completed by May 2005, the original date for sea trials. At this time the tri-national PAAMS Project Office responsible

for developing Sea Viper was concentrating on the alternative Franco-Italian version of the AAW system. There were delays to both the Sea Viper command and control software as well as the technically advanced Sampson MFR. By early 2005 the performance of Sampson's gallium arsenide transmit/receive modules was sufficiently below expectations to require redesign that further delayed the sea trials.

For the trials *Longbow* had two CMS consoles that could be used to fire missiles in the local configuration that the destroyers would use in the case of loss of the ship's CMS. By the end of June 2005 Setting to Work of the CMS consoles, METOC system and a fully representative DTS had both been completed on *Longbow.* At the same time, Setting to Work had also been completed at the Maritime Integration and Support Centre, with its eight-console CMS, allowing work to start on integrating the whole combat system. This would enable the Sampson MFR prototype P3 to be tested and integrated with more elements of the combat system.

Following a redesign of Sampson MFR transmit/receive modules, *Longbow* undertook radar-tracking trials around the Isle of Wight before departing for a firing programme in the Mediterranean starting in early 2008. At the *Centre d'Essais de Lancement Missiles*, *Longbow* was moored to the 11m-diameter turret buoy of a Catenary Anchor Leg Mooring deep-water anchoring system. The ground mooring conditions were not ideal, so this sophisticated anchoring system was required to

ABOVE LEFT Sea trials platform *Longbow* after conversion and outfitting with Sea Viper trials equipment. *(BMT Group)*

ABOVE *Longbow* Catenary Anchor Leg Mooring turret buoy near Toulon. *(BMT Group)*

ABOVE **Mirach 100/5 target vehicle.** *(Selex Galileo)*

ABOVE RIGHT **Aster missile successfully fired from *Longbow*, 17 August 2010.**

achieve the necessary precise positioning.

Aster-15 and Aster-30 missiles had already been proved and qualified in 2002 and 2003 as part of French missile systems. On the range in June 2008 and February 2009, trials on *Longbow* successfully demonstrated Sea Viper tracking multiple supersonic and subsonic targets. A programme of missile firings also showed the effectiveness of the system. The third and final pre-qualification trial was in May 2009, with the firing of a two-missile salvo against a Mirach 100/5 low-altitude manoeuvring target. However, in a major setback to the Sea Viper delivery programme, the missiles failed to intercept the target.

The trial was repeated, again unsuccessfully, in November 2009. Analysis showed that neither the Sampson MFR nor the command and control system was responsible for the fault. It was later attributed to engineering changes during missile manufacturing that detrimentally affected its structural integrity. In June 2010, after rectification of the fault, a salvo of two Aster-30 missiles from *Longbow* successfully intercepted the low-altitude Mirach, despite the target executing an evasive high-g 'dog-leg' manoeuvre.

Contractor's sea trials (CSTs)

The CSTs are a series of trials undertaken to test the basic operation of all aspects of the ship's hull and systems. Trials of the combat system and live firings, however, are undertaken once the warship has been handed over to the

RN. These CSTs are carried out in parallel with, but separate from, Sea Viper trials and the land-based combat system trials.

On 18 July 2007 *Daring* sailed on the first set (Stage 1.1) of CST. These trials were primarily to demonstrate the effectiveness of this first all-electric warship. It was also used to test the 'ship' part of 'warship' – the platform itself including propulsion systems, controls, key weapons engineering systems, navigation, radars and gyros, as well as the habitability of the ship including the galley, cabins, sewage treatment plant, ventilation and lighting. As the First of Class, additional structural tests were performed. For instance, MCG firings were carried out to evaluate the effects on the ship's structure.

During the four-week trials period, *Daring* sailed approximately 3,600NM (6,600km) using an average of 35m³ of fuel per day, and refuelled only once. Despite having a displacement 50% greater than the Type 42 destroyers, this fuel consumption is a quarter of that of its predecessor. Indeed, *Daring* can achieve 11 knots (20km/h) with only 5% of the installed power of a Type 42.

The speed target was 28 knots and, with her 40MW propulsion system, *Daring* attained this in only 70sec from a standing start. After just over 120sec a maximum speed was reached. A crash stop from 30 knots (55.6km/h) was achieved in about 5.5 ship lengths. The trials also showed *Daring*'s manoeuvrability by performing a full turning circle – or tactical diameter – of less than three ship's lengths.

Between 30 March and 2 May 2008 Stage

1.2 trials were performed. These involved trials
of the LRR, demonstration of the navigation
system, weapon alignment tests, endurance
tests and MCG blast trials.

The fully integrated communications
system (FICS) was tested to its limits between
26 August and 22 September 2008 during
Daring's Stage 1.3 sea trials, with 30 or more
operators using all aspects of the system
simultaneously from locations throughout the
ship. Communications were tested with other
vessels and with shore-based operators.
This demonstrated that the FICS could
seamlessly operate and manage a full range
of communication frequencies, including

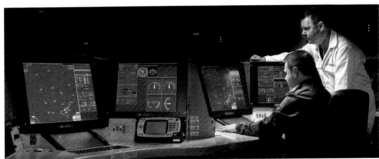

video conferencing by satellite. The ship's
company used this trial as an opportunity to
conduct familiarisation and training activities in
preparation for the transfer of the vessel to
the RN.

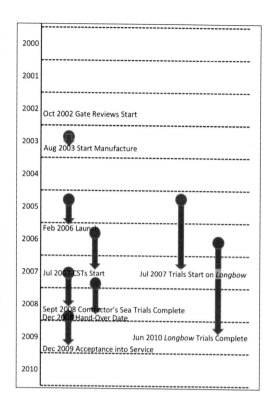

Oct 2002 Gate Reviews Start

Aug 2003 Start Manufacture

Feb 2006 Launch

Jul 2007 OCSTs Start   Jul 2007 Trials Start on *Longbow*

Sept 2008 Contractor's Sea Trials Complete
Dec 2008 Hand-Over Date

Jun 2010 *Longbow* Trials Complete

Dec 2009 Acceptance into Service

JACKSPEAK

To fully prepare
them for
operational duties,
RN warships
undertake intensive
Operational Sea
Training exercises
that are dubbed
a 'work-up'. The
exercises climax in
a realistic major air,
surface and sub-
surface exercise
on the penultimate
day, nicknamed
The Thursday War.

Naval trials

HMS *Daring* was handed over to the RN
on 10 December 2008, and exchanged
her blue ensign for the navy's white ensign.
She travelled to Portsmouth, her home port,
to begin a period of further (Stage 2) trials that
could not be undertaken by the contractor.

HMS *Daring* was commissioned by HRH
the Countess of Wessex at a ceremony held
in Portsmouth on 23 July 2009 and entered
the list of active ships of the RN.

Further trials were undertaken to bring
the ship to full operational readiness, such
as undertaking high-speed manoeuvres and
communications exercises in conjunction
with other vessels. These ensured that HMS
Daring was prepared to undertake her first
period of intensive Operational Sea Training
in the spring of 2010. These realistic
training exercises test whether the warship
and the ship's company can perform
operational duties.

As the First of Class many lessons were
learnt during these exercises about the
operation of the destroyers in front-line
deployments. After further work, including
the fitting of the Phalanx close-in weapon
system (CIWS), HMS *Daring* endured a
further eight weeks of Operational Sea
Training exercises. She achieved a 'very
satisfactory' score (most ships are graded
'satisfactory').

For operational reasons, Sea Viper firings
at sea from a Type 45 destroyer were first
successfully demonstrated by the Second of
Class, HMS *Dauntless*, on 1 October 2010,
with a direct hit on a target flying at a speed of

**LEFT Ship's company just before their ship was
commissioned as HMS *Daring*.** *(Crown Copyright,
2009 LA(Phot) Christopher Browne)*

**BELOW Band of the Royal Marines, Portsmouth,
playing at the commissioning ceremony of HMS
Daring, 23 July 2009.** *(Clare Parker)*

200m/sec and an altitude of 9km. HMS *Daring* successfully engaged a target with Sea Viper on 17 May 2011.

Now fully operational, during October 2011 HMS *Daring* took part in the first major NATO exercise for a Type 45 destroyer. To demonstrate her powerful capabilities, HMS *Daring* was charged with defending the skies around the USS *Enterprise* and her escorts. On her return journey, HMS *Daring* paid a goodwill visit to New York.

The first operational deployment of a Type 45 destroyer started on 11 January 2012 when HMS *Daring* left for the Gulf by way of the Suez Canal as part of the long-standing RN presence in the Middle East. HMS *Daring* and

ABOVE **HMS** *Daring* **visits New York.** *(Crown Copyright, 2010 Kristen Whalen Somody)*

BELOW **HMS** *Daring* **passes through the Suez Canal.** *(Crown Copyright, 2012 LA(Phot) Keith Morgan)*

her company were principally deployed as part of the Combined Maritime Task Forces where, with other partner nations, she conducted tasks ranging from maritime security, counter-piracy and the wider maritime security effort dedicated to maintaining stability in the region. During the seven-month deployment HMS *Daring* travelled 35,000NM (64,900km).

Follow-on build

A year into *Daring*'s production, work began on blocks for the second ship, *Dauntless*, in Portsmouth and Govan. By this time Govan's facilities had been upgraded so *Dauntless* and all subsequent Type 45 destroyers were assembled on the newly improved slipway at Govan and launched from there. During the building of *Daring*, Blocks B and C were joined in Scotstoun to form a 2,568-tonne 'megablock'. Blocks A, B, C and D for subsequent vessels were all fabricated at Govan and joined on the slipway to form the hull. The height restriction that prevented *Daring* from being launched at Scotstoun with

TOP **Block C being moved behind Block D on slipway.** *(BAE Systems)*

ABOVE **Blocks being joined on slipway.** *(BAE Systems)*

ABOVE *Duncan*, **the sixth and last Type 45 destroyer, launched from Govan.** *(Crown Copyright, 2010 POA(Phot) Ian Arthur)*

BELOW **HMS *Duncan*, sixth and final Type 45 destroyer.** *(Dave Taskis)*

her foremast fitted did not apply at Govan, where ships were launched with the foremast in position.

The production schedule was for the five follow-on ships to be started on an annual basis and launched approximately 28 months later. After launch, the ships crossed the River Clyde to the Scotstoun's Elderslie dry dock for outfitting.

As the class progressed, efficiency increased and more outfitting was undertaken ashore during the building of the blocks. This reduced the time taken for outfitting at Scotstoun. The CST period was also reduced; after the trials of *Daring* and *Dauntless* the remaining ships of the class only required two, not three, periods of CST.

Duncan, the sixth, and last, Type 45 destroyer to be built was handed over to the RN in March 2013.

Chapter Two

Anatomy of the hull and infrastructure

Type 45 destroyers are expected to go in harm's way. Under the demanding conditions of both naval warfare and a hostile maritime environment the destroyers must nevertheless be capable of performing a wide range of duties. Furthermore, the warship must also act as a home for the ship's complement for weeks at a time.

OPPOSITE Marine engineer on HMS *Diamond* controls the ship's propulsion and electrical systems during exercises. *(BAE Systems)*

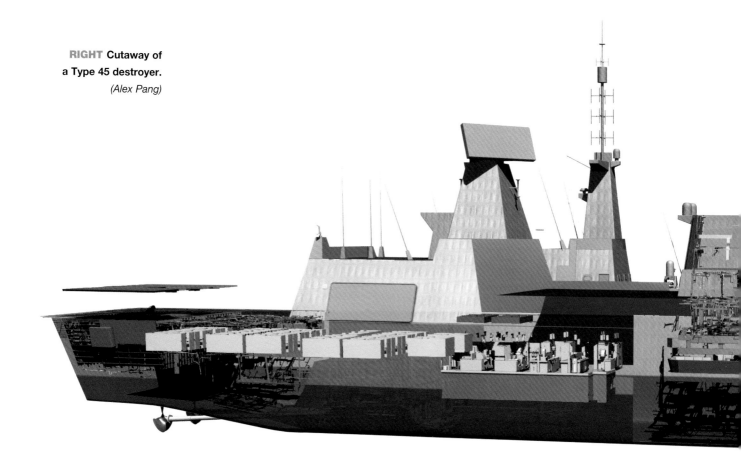

Overview of HMS *Daring*

HMS *Daring* and her sister Type 45 destroyers can be distinguished by their large, pyramidal foremast topped by the large, almost spherical Sampson MFR. The hull and superstructure present large flat areas that slope gently. Any openings in the hull and superstructure are covered so that they are contiguous with the ship's structure, so barely noticeable. These clean lines are emphasised by the lack of extraneous external equipment. Although these features are aesthetically pleasing, this form is driven by function. They represent 'stealth' measures to make the warship less easily detected by radar. It is not possible to make an 8,000-tonne vessel invisible, but the signature can be significantly

reduced to make detection more difficult and the ship's countermeasures more effective.

The highest deck that runs the complete length of the warship is called 1-Deck. Decks below this level are within the hull of the ship and numbered sequentially 2-Deck, 3-Deck, 4-Deck, etc. The ship's waterline is approximately at the level of 3-Deck. Above 1-Deck lie the superstructure and mast structures, and their decks are named

01-Deck, 02-Deck, etc, to 09-Deck – this being the highest deck of the foremast that supports the Sampson MFR antenna.

Horizontally the ship is divided into 17 sections. These are given letters, from A, at the bow, through to M, the sternmost section. The letter I is omitted, to avoid confusion with number 1. Within the hull, the vertical boundaries of the sections are watertight bulkheads whose

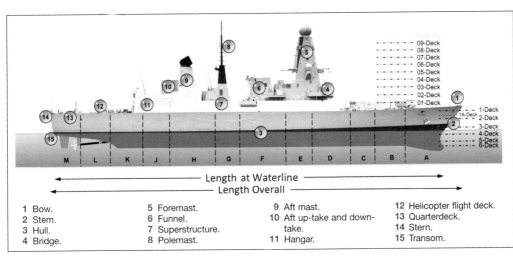

1 Bow.	5 Foremast.
2 Stem.	6 Funnel.
3 Hull.	7 Superstructure.
4 Bridge.	8 Polemast.

9 Aft mast.	12 Helicopter flight deck.
10 Aft up-take and down-take.	13 Quarterdeck.
	14 Stern.
11 Hangar.	15 Transom.

LEFT Key nomenclature indicated on HMS *Daring*. (Author)

ABOVE **Dome for medium frequency sonar seen when Type 45 destroyer is in dry dock: (a) newly installed** (BAE Systems); **(b) after five years, showing effectiveness of anti-fouling** (BAE Systems).

JACKSPEAK

The grey naval paint thickly applied to RN warships is nicknamed *'Pusser's Crabfat'*, because it was a similar colour to the thick jelly used to treat body lice ('crabs'); any material issued to the RN was termed 'Pusser's' from the original term purser. Incidentally, it is because of the colour of their uniforms that RAF officers are colloquially called 'crabs' by naval personnel.

openings can be sealed to prevent the spread of flooding should the warship sustain damage. The naval terminology used in this book is explained in more detail in Appendix 1.

Like all RN warships, the destroyers are painted a traditional grey colour, but low solar absorption paint has been used. In bright sunshine this type of paint absorbs less heat than normal paint, so the structure contributes less to the ship's infrared signature. The hull has the same grey paint down to the black boot-topping – an area that is continually exposed to both seawater and air – that is particularly prone to fouling by marine growths.

Beneath the waterline anti-fouling is used to impede corrosion and to inhibit marine growths, both of which increase the ship's propulsive resistance and its fuel consumption. The environmentally friendly anti-fouling contains none of the biocides that were a feature of previous generations. It is also durable, requiring fewer expensive periods in dry dock to renew it.

The weather decks are protected by a non-toxic, fire-retardant, hard-wearing epoxy resin

reinforced with Glassflake particles that ensure the surface coating is anti-slip. This enhanced protection system is anti-corrosive and forms an impact-resistant barrier.

The bow

A Type 45 destroyer's forward weather deck is uncluttered, with no equipment between the jackstaff and the breakwater (some 20m further aft) that protects the base of the MCG. Much of the equipment traditionally accommodated on the weather deck is contained within the enclosed forecastle deck below. This is a stealth measure but also protects the equipment and facilitates its operation in rough weather. The deck encloses two anchor winches, two five-tonne mooring capstans, stainless steel bollards and fairleads. A large seamanship opening leads from the enclosed deck up on to the weather deck. To withstand the pounding of heavy seas this is sturdily constructed of composite material. It is large enough to accommodate personnel wearing breathing apparatus and its operation is hydraulically assisted.

When at anchor in harbour Type 45 destroyers are secured by the central bow anchor, whose anchor chain passes through the central hawse-pipe. The main anchor is sited slightly aft of the stem on the starboard side. The chain for this anchor passes down to 2-Deck, to a hawse-pipe on the starboard side.

Beneath the forecastle deck are stores, ballast

LEFT **Uncluttered foredeck of HMS *Daring*. The forecastle seamanship hatch and the mine-lookout position in the hull are both open.** (Airfix)

LEFT Cutaway diagram of the bow. *(Alex Pang/Author)*

1 Seamanship opening.
2 Bow anchor.
3 Enclosed forecastle deck.
4 Foredeck.
5 Sonar dome.
6 Main anchor.
7 Breakwater.
8 Medium-calibre gun.
9 Spaces for future use.
10 Sea Viper silos.

JACKSPEAK

The central anchor-chain hawser at the bow is called the 'Bullring', as the anchor-chain passing through it secures the ship in the same way that ropes attached to a nose-ring are used to control a bull.

tanks and the dome for the medium-frequency sonar (MFS). In the event of head-on collision there is a collision bulkhead to prevent flooding.

On the weather deck, just forward of the superstructure, there are additional bollards and fairleads for securing cables and ropes during operations such as berthing.

ABOVE View of enclosed forecastle (looking aft) as sailors from HMS *Defender* are briefed before dropping anchor. *(Crown Copyright, 2012 HMS Defender)*

LEFT Enclosed forecastle (looking forward) on HMS *Defender* as sailors align the anchor chain. *(Crown Copyright, 2012 HMS Defender)*

BELOW Sailors securing ropes to a pair of bollards during berthing. *(Crown Copyright, 2011 LA(Phot) Kyle Heller)*

ABOVE **Captain Robinson on the bridge of HMS** *Daring. (Crown Copyright, 2012 LA(Phot) Keith Morgan)*

ABOVE **Commanding Officer's chair on the bridge of HMS** *Diamond. (Daniel Ferro)*

LEFT **Starboard part of the bridge including the Commanding Officer's chair.** *(Daniel Ferro)*

The bridge

During normal duties the destroyer is conned from the bridge by the Captain unless this duty is delegated to the Officer of the Watch. The bridge is equipped with all displays and consoles necessary for steering, control of the engines, navigation, communications and meteorological and oceanographic equipment.

Other members of the on-watch staff on the bridge include the Officer of the Watch, the

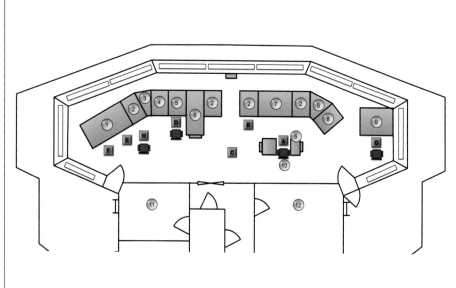

Schematic of bridge layout. *(Author from BAE Systems information)*

 1 Chart table.
 2 Navigation multifunction console.
 3 Port corner console.
 4 Platform management system console.
 5 Navigation multifunction display.
 6 Navigation system control console.
 7 Officer of the Watch multi-purpose console.
 8 Combat system console.
 9 Communications console.
10 Commanding Officer's position.
11 Navigation Officer's cabin.
12 Combined chartroom and METOC office.
 A Commanding Officer.
 B Navigating Officer.
 C Officer of the Watch.
 D Quartermaster.
 E Second Officer of the Watch.
 F Boatswain's Mate.
 G Tactical communicator.
 H Senior Officer's chair (provision made in design).

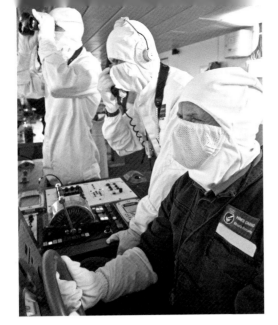

Navigating Officer and the Quartermaster, who steers the ship and controls the engines and propulsion system. Although the bridge is fully electronic there are still traditional navigation charts available. When the ship is at action stations bridge functions are undertaken in the Operations Complex and the Ship Control Centre.

The Captain retains the ultimate responsibility for the ship at all times, so his quarters are located between the bridge and the Operations Complex. The Captain's day room is a combination of office and a space where the Captain can entertain visitors. When embarked, the Commander of the Task Force has a small cabin adjacent to the Captain's cabin.

The navigation system Type NavS1

The navigation system is based on an Electronic Chart, Display and Information System (ECDIS). This is an International Maritime Organisation-approved commercial system modified for use on warships by the inclusion of security-classified information called Additional Military Layers. The system incorporates worldwide electronic navigation charts, including commercial S57 charts (where available), electronic versions of hard-copy charts supplied by Admiralty Raster Chart Services as well as classified military charts. The two Type 1047 I-band navigation radars provide information about surface features and vessels nearby. Their 2.95m antennas are mounted on the port side of the foremast and aft starboard side of the hangar roof in order that their signals can be combined to give 360° coverage. These

radars are also fitted with C-band Identification Friend or Foe (IFF) Type RRB that enables them to be used for helicopter control. The navigation system can also take inputs from the Type 1048 E/F-band search radar, the 3.84m antenna of which is mounted centrally on the forward face of the foremast. The navigation radars and search radar all rotate at 28rpm. The navigation system uses an automatic radar-plotting aid that detects radar tracks and predicts the closest point of approach and the closest time of approach to the ship of tracked objects. Operators can select the information

ABOVE LEFT

Helmsman (foreground) and officers on the bridge of HMS *Daring* at action stations. *(BAE Systems)*

ABOVE Captain Robinson briefing distinguished visitors in his day room. *(Crown Copyright, 2012 LA(Phot) Keith Morgan)*

LEFT Navigation displays of (a) navigation radars *(Raytheon Anschütz)*; **(b) electronic chart display and information system** *(Raytheon Anschütz)*.

JACKSPEAK

The origin of the term 'log' dates back to the days when the ship's speed was determined by throwing a piece of wood over the side – literally a log – and timing how long it took to travel the length of the ship.

JACKSPEAK

Visual identification still forms a cornerstone of warship navigation as, for many purposes, there has yet to be an improvement on what Jack refers to as the Mk1 Eyeball.

BELOW Officers on the bridge of HMS *Diamond* take visual bearings and scan the environs with binoculars. *(Crown Copyright, 2010 LA(Phot) Ben Sutton)*

displayed from pure radar information, a chart display or displays that overlay these two types of information.

The identification of commercial ships in the vicinity is facilitated by the integrated automatic identification system. This system, mandated by the International Maritime Organisation, is a commercial maritime data-link operating at very high frequency (VHF) and fitted to all ships over 300 tonnes. The signal provides information about the ship's name, position, heading and speed, and is intended both to avoid collisions and to assist coastguards with traffic management in congested waters such as the English Channel.

The navigation system control console on the bridge is the Navigating Officer's main interface with the navigation system. There are four navigation multifunction consoles on the bridge that share similar hardware with the navigation system control console, including the 23in liquid crystal display. There is also a navigation multifunction console in the Operations Room and one in the Chart Room. The latter is connected to the voyage data recorder.

In addition to the navigation multifunction consoles there are navigation multifunction displays with smaller 10in liquid crystal displays at two positions on the bridge, the bridge wings, Chart Room and positions throughout the ship such as the flight director's caboose.

The navigation system receives navigational data from a number of sources through two identical data distribution units. The data gathered includes:

- Pitch, roll and ship's heading data from the two maritime inertial navigation systems, each comprising three laser-ring gyroscopes mounted orthogonally.
- Ship's heading from a magnet compass.
- Ship's geographical position from two P(Y) coded global positioning system (GPS) receivers.
- Ship's geographical position from a LORAN and differential GPS combination receiver.
- Depth of the seabed from the echo-sounder, which has two transducers mounted on the hull, one low frequency (12kHz) for deep water and one high frequency (200kHz) for shallow water.
- Longitudinal and transverse speed through the water from the dual-axis electro-magnetic log system.

The navigation system is fully integrated with the combat system, to which it supplies important data. While the processing of navigational data and its distribution to other systems is highly automated, the navigation of the ship relies on traditional seamanship skills. This means that there is still great importance placed on verifying navigational data with visual identification and manually obtained bearings of navigational features and other vessels.

The masts and superstructure

The foremast is a signature feature of Type 45 destroyers that makes them instantly recognisable. The Sampson MFR Type 1045 mounted on top of the foremast largely determines the mast's size and shape. However, the mast also supports several sensors and communications antennas. The equipment associated with the antennas is largely accommodated within this spacious structure.

The length of the superstructure is almost exactly half the length of the Type 45 destroyer. It includes the bridge, masts, funnel structure, boat bays and the hangar. The main operational superstructure weather deck is 01-Deck. It comprises port and starboard open sidedecks running from beneath the bridge wings aft for some 45m. The sidedecks are over 4.5m wide and linked by a 7m-wide cross-deck

ABOVE Cutaway of foremast. *(Alex Pang)*

aft of the funnel. Inboard of the sidedecks is the superstructure, but a 1m-high bulwark defines the seaward extent of the sidedecks. The bulwarks are not only protective but also reduce the radar cross-section of the ship. They have scuppers at deck level to drain water overboard. Longitudinal sections of the bulwarks can be lowered to allow access to 01-Deck for

1 Sampson Type 1045 MFR.	**7** EOSP (port and starboard).	
2 RESM antennae.	**8** Inmarsat antenna.	
3 Satcom antenna (port and starboard).	**9** METOC antenna.	
4 Type 1048 antenna (search).	**10** Bridge.	
5 Communications yardarms.	**11** Bridge wing (port and starboard).	
6 Type 1047 antenna (navigation).		

ABOVE Foremast and bridge roof sensors and communications antennas. *(Author/Dan Grant photo)*

1	Bridge and bridge wing.
2	Foremast.
3	RAS highpoint.
4	Down-take.
5	Removable bulwarks.
6	SCG platform.
7	Funnel structure.
8	Forward up-take.
9	Phalanx sponson.
10	Polemast.
11	LRR mast.
12	Aft up-take.
13	Boat bay.
14	Hangar.

LEFT Superstructure elements. *(Author/USN photo, 2012 Thomas Epps)*

RIGHT Starboard Phalanx close-in weapon system on its sponson from 01-Deck. *(Dan Grant)*

replenishment at sea, the launch of life rafts and loading of stores directly from the jetty.

There are six doors that access the internal superstructure spaces from 01-Deck. There are also many doors on the superstructure that lead to lockers and compartments for stowing equipment such as decoy round magazines, small-calibre ammunition magazines and the

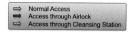

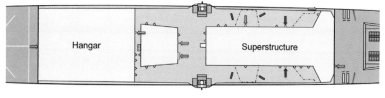

ABOVE Access to superstructure from 01-Deck. *(Author)*

RIGHT Gastight and watertight doors to the lift (left) and into the superstructure (right), with a ramp (foreground) that allows stores to be wheeled over the sill of the lift door. *(Airfix)*

gun crew's shelter. All superstructure doors are watertight. There are four moveable high-points so the ship can accept the transfer of fuel and stores, both of which come aboard on 01-Deck from replenishment ships.

Superstructure weapons on both port and starboard sides are identical: on each side of 01-Deck is a Phalanx CIWS and two decoy launchers, whereas a small-calibre gun (SCG) is mounted on a platform either side at 02-Deck level.

Access

When in port, the main access to the ship is by a brow to the flight deck that is guarded by the Quartermaster's staff. There is an alternative brow position to the foredeck. There are also doors in the hull port and starboard at 1-Deck, sited almost exactly midships, that lead to the Quartermaster's lobby. Whether at anchor or under way, these are the entrances for visitors and ship's company alike who arrive by boat and climb the Accommodation Ladder. The Accommodation Ladder is normally stored within a stowage space running aft along the ship from the hull doorway. The stowage is behind a 10m-long, vertically opening closure hinged at the top. When needed, the ladder hinges downward to the horizontal, and the aft end is lowered to the sea's surface.

There are several doorways giving access to the superstructure from the flight deck, the foredeck and 01-Deck. All these doorways are watertight, but three on 01-Deck are also gastight and are the only doorways used at action stations, when chemical, biological, radiological and nuclear (CBRN) warfare is possible. Two of the doors allow entrance through airlocks and the third through a cleansing station (for personnel who have been the subject of such an attack). There is also an airlock and a cleansing station at the forward end of the hangar for personnel on duty in the hangar and flight deck. The opening to the central stores lift on 01-Deck is also gastight and watertight. Four large springs assist personnel in opening the lift's large doorway. All personnel doorways have hinges adapted to cope with the sloping superstructure.

Within the warship the main passageway on

2-Deck runs from the Sylver launcher forward to the enclosed quarterdeck aft – a distance of over 90m. This passageway is similar to the shorter 1-Deck passageway above it. Both the passageways have a generous minimum clear width and height of 1.25m and 2.1m respectively, to allow easy passage of personnel and equipment. Even the minor and secondary passageways have a minimum clear width and height of 0.95m and 2.1m.

All internal bulkhead doors are watertight and have a clear height of 1.94m to allow access to firefighters wearing helmets. When attack by CBRN agents is anticipated the ship can be partitioned into separate, gastight zones by closing certain gastight bulkhead doors. The bulkhead doors are of a new design that can be opened and closed with a single-lever operating mechanism but, when closed, are clipped at several points. The design has been made possible by new silicon polymer seals that need much less pressure to compress than rubber seals.

The regulations regarding doors reflect the fact that warships 'go in harm's way' and may sustain action damage. As a result, there are no doorways through watertight bulkheads on decks below 2-Deck. On lower decks (3-Deck and below), moving between compartments in adjacent watertight sections necessitates climbing to 2-Deck, passing through a watertight doorway to the next section and descending again to the required deck.

Vertical access to decks is through hatches leading to ladders. The hatches have also been redesigned to have a single-lever action and are counter-balanced to make them easy to open.

LEFT **Main 2-Deck passageway.** *(Crown Copyright, 2012 HMS Defender)*

JACKSPEAK

The main passageway is often referred to as the 'Main Drag', as it is at the heart of the ship.

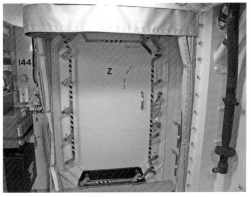

LEFT **Watertight doorway where 2-Deck passageway passes through a watertight bulkhead.** *(Crown Copyright, 2012 HMS Defender)*

Despite the larger passageways, the policy for equipment dimensions remains the same as for previous classes. Wherever possible, no dimension should exceed 760mm and any equipment should weigh less than 50kg,

BOTTOM LEFT
Watertight and gastight doorway for 2-Deck passageway with watertight doorway in the distance. Note the bulks of wood for damage control purposes in the passageway between the doorways. *(Crown Copyright, 2012 HMS Defender)*

LEFT **Hatchway in the 2-Deck passageway on HMS *Defender* leading to a ladder to lower decks.** *(Crown Copyright, 2012 HMS Defender)*

as transporting larger and heavier equipment along the passageways would require special equipment. Equipment and parts exceeding these dimensions and weight, such as gas turbine modules and diesel engines, require pre-planned removal and replacement routes. Such routes may include removal through down-takes or involve areas of deck that can be opened temporarily. Temporary openings may be bolted plates or, alternatively, 'soft patches' – areas designed to be cut out and then re-welded later.

The main stores lift services the decks from replenishment areas on 01-Deck down to 5-Deck. It transports victuals and food stores to the main dry provisions store, cool-rooms and cold-rooms. The cool-rooms and cold-room are accessed from an insulated airlock that also serves as a temperature-controlled storage (5° ± 1°C) for dairy produce. Thermal curtains are incorporated in its entrance and across its storage racks. The airlock leads to a potato cool-room (6° ± 1°C), a fruit and vegetables cool-room (5° ± 1°C), and the cold-room (-20° ± 2°C). Thermal curtains are fitted across the entrances to these compartments. When food from the stores is needed in the

galley, the lift can deliver it to a 2-Deck lobby, conveniently adjacent to the galley. This system avoids a great deal of the manual labour that was needed on earlier warships to strike down and distribute stores, in particular victuals that have a high turnover. The lift is also used for transporting equipment spares to and from their stores.

The galley and dining halls

Unlike previous RN ships of destroyer size, there is only one galley to provide all the meals for the whole ship's complement. In order that the chefs can prepare and cook the large numbers of meals that have to be served, the galley has state-of-the-art equipment. The galley is sited between the junior ratings' and senior ratings' dining halls. The Wardroom Steward's Pantry above is served by a 'dumb waiter' lift. As a consequence, all meals (apart from the Captain's) are served within a few metres of the galley. Special arrangements are made to keep meals hot for the Captain and any guests dining in his day room. The whole ship's company has the same meals, although

JACKSPEAK

To *victual* (pronounced 'vittle') a warship is to take on board food and provisions. Food is consequently referred to as victuals, so Jack uses this word to indicate eating.

FAR LEFT Galley on HMS *Defender*. *(Crown Copyright, 2012 HMS Defender)*

LEFT Chefs prepare meals in HMS *Diamond*'s galley. *(Crown Copyright, 2013 PO(Phot) Paul Punter)*

FAR LEFT Junior ratings' dining hall on HMS *Defender*. *(Crown Copyright, 2012 HMS Defender)*

LEFT Servery for the junior ratings' dining hall on HMS *Defender*. *(Crown Copyright, 2012 HMS Defender)*

officers traditionally pay an extra-messing allowance for small luxuries such as real orange juice and a wider selection of cheeses.

The junior ratings' dining hall has seating for 40 diners. A range of dishes is served at a canteen-style servery immediately outside the hall. Food is available at times to suit the watch system of the ship. During peak meal times, ratings return their used plates to a scullery to one side of the dining hall where they are cleaned by junior ratings selected on a rota basis.

Accommodation

O n early generations of RN warships, groups of sailors lived in messes that were used for sleeping, eating and recreation. However, to recruit and retain the high-calibre,

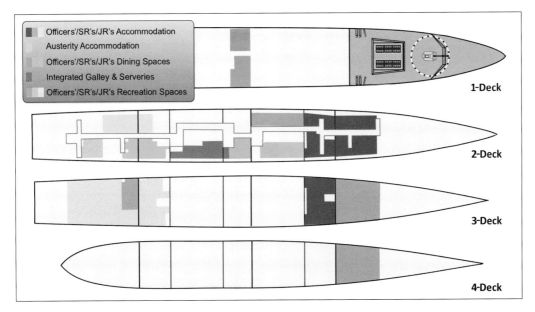

Officers'/SR's/JR's Accommodation
Austerity Accommodation
Officers'/SR's/JR's Dining Spaces
Integrated Galley & Serveries
Officers'/SR's/JR's Recreation Spaces

1-Deck

2-Deck

3-Deck

4-Deck

LEFT Disposition of officers', senior ratings' and junior ratings' accommodation and living spaces on HMS *Daring*. *(Author from BAE Systems information)*

JACKSPEAK

In the days of 'wooden wall' sailing warships there were no toilets, so the crew relieved themselves at the bow (or head) of the vessel. Toilets are consequently referred to as 'the heads'.

diverse personnel necessary to operate a state-of-the-art, complex warship, it is essential to provide modern facilities. In a departure from traditional practice, there are dedicated spaces for each function, with facilities that meet the very latest RN standards for crew comfort. In addition, the overall *per capita* accommodation space is 40% greater than that of other existing warships. HMS *Daring* was the first RN warship to be truly gender neutral with, for instance, individual facilities for all 44 showers, 54 heads and 100 washbasins.

All cabins on the ship are fully carpeted and outfitted with wipe-clean furniture. Junior ratings

share six-berth cabins. The berths are at least 1.97m long, recognising that the average height of the nation's men and women has increased over recent decades and is predicted to grow further during the ship's life. The berths are at least 850mm wide and arranged as three sets, two tiers high (in previous warships, ratings slept in three-tier bunks). The two-tier arrangement provides personal spaces with sufficient headroom to enable occupants to sit up to read or use electronic equipment. Each berth has a personal reading light, electrical sockets for personal electronic equipment and Internet connection. For security reasons, Internet is only available for authorised ship's laptops, all of which have appropriate in-built security measures. Each rating has a personal locker, drop-down cupboard and drawer as part of their berth. The cabin also has a wardrobe for uniform and plain clothes.

HMS *Daring* was designed for worldwide operations, therefore her heating, ventilation and air conditioning system has been designed to ensure crew comfort in temperature extremes from the Poles to the Gulf.

Some senior ratings' cabins are adjacent to the junior ratings' cabins, although most of the senior ratings' accommodation is forward. Senior ratings occupy either twin-berth cabins or, where they have greater departmental responsibilities, single-berth cabins. Officers (except those under training) have single-berth cabins that double as offices for their occupants, so are equipped with desks and filing cabinets. The beds can be folded away

to become seating. These cabins also have integral washbasins.

The ship's complement is 191 but there are berths for about 235 to allow for additional personnel such as an Embarked Military Force, complete with their weapons and equipment. Some of these troops will use austerity accommodation. Although it is austere compared to the standards of the rest of the ship, the accommodation, in ten three-tier bunks with single personal lockers, is similar to the standard accommodation on Type 42 destroyers. This accommodation is only intended for short-term use.

Recreational spaces

The junior ratings' and the senior ratings' recreational areas are similar and are located near their respective berths. On the Type 45 destroyers all ranks will benefit from dedicated and spacious recreation areas comprising three interconnecting but separate compartments, with comfortable seating for 86. They provide a space where all ratings, male and female, can relax. Whereas the old messing system was based on the speciality of the ratings, this system allows all ratings to meet together, engendering a wider team spirit.

The main section has bar facilities, including beer coolers. The adjacent space has audio-visual entertainment with equipment such as TVs and DVD players, and the final section is a quiet zone for studying or reading and provides facilities for making tea and coffee. It is possible to partition these areas in order that there can be TV areas separate from social areas and the quiet zone. Before HMS *Daring* entered service there was some concern that the system might result in loss of mess-deck camaraderie. Mainly because of the large and well-appointed recreation space this has not proved to be the case.

It is vital that RN crews can stay fit while they are at sea. While many RN ships currently carry pieces of exercise equipment, HMS *Daring* is the first RN warship to be designed with a dedicated, permanent fitness centre (gym) on

ABOVE Ratings of HMS *Defender* in the junior ratings' recreation area.
(Crown Copyright, 2012 HMS Defender*)*

BELOW Gym equipment in the fitness centre on HMS *Daring*.
(Crown Copyright, 2012 LA(Phot) Keith Morgan)

ABOVE Royal Marines exercising on HMS *Daring*'s 01-Deck. *(Crown Copyright, 2012 LA(Phot) Keith Morgan)*

BELOW HMS *Defender*'s Wardroom. *(Crown Copyright, 2012 HMS Defender)*

BELOW RIGHT HMS *Defender*'s Wardroom Anteroom. *(Crown Copyright, 2012 HMS Defender)*

board. The gym, available for the whole ship's company, is located beneath the junior ratings' cabins on 4-Deck. The gym is provided with the normal range of fitness equipment found ashore, such as running machines, step machines, cross-trainers, spinners, bikes, rowing machines and multi-gym equipment but, because of the effect of the ship's motion, free-weights are not provided! Of course, the ship's company can also stay fit by jogging around the generous flight deck (ten laps of the flight deck equates to running one kilometre) or the 01-Deck space.

On 1-Deck, close to the key control compartments, are the Wardroom and the Wardroom Anteroom. The Wardroom is where officers take their meals. It will normally seat 30 officers but can seat 40 should this be necessary. Meals are delivered by a lift from the galley and served by Wardroom stewards.

The Wardroom Anteroom is the area where the officers may relax. It is equipped with easy chairs and a bar. There is also a movie projector and screen to show the traditional weekly movies.

The integrated electric propulsion system (IEPS)

Type 45 destroyers were the first major warships to have an IEPS, with propellers rotated directly by electric motors. Of course, in addition to propulsion, the warship uses electrical power to operate all the ship's equipment, and for services such as lighting, heating and air conditioning, and these systems are linked to the IEPS. Power is produced by four prime movers – two gas turbines and two diesels – each connected to its own alternator that generates the electrical power. The alternators operate

at 4.16kV, the voltage used by the propulsion equipment, and transformers reduce this to the traditional 440V required by the ship's combat system and services equipment.

The IEPS comprises two identical, but cross-connected, electrical systems controlled by the electrical power management system (EPMS). The duplication of power and propulsion systems marks a return to previous RN practice that increases flexibility, availability and ship survivability.

The two halves of the electric propulsion system are physically separated into port and starboard systems, with each driving the appropriate propeller in normal operation. Each half comprises:

- A WR-21 advanced cycle gas turbine, rated at 25MW, connected to a 4.16kV/21MW alternator that together are known as a gas turbine alternator operating at 3,600rpm.
- A diesel engine directly coupled to a 4.16kV/2MW alternator (together known as a diesel alternator).
- A pulse-width modulated converter consisting of three channels of five phases each.
- A 15-phase AIM rated at 20MW at 165rpm.
- A 2MW 4.16kV/440V ship's services transformer.
- Two harmonic filters, one for 4.16kV and one for 440V.
- Two switchboards, one for 4.16kV and one for 440V.
- Three dynamic breaking resistors.
- Two main shaft lines each rotating a five-bladed propeller at the same speed as the motors.

At full power the two systems operate independently but with the power split between them. The system is, however, extremely flexible, with different configurations being adopted depending upon the power required and the degree of resilience to damage that is appropriate. For instance, at low speed in peacetime the total ship's electrical power can be provided by a single gas turbine.

The principal source of electric power is the two GTAs that are powered by the revolutionary WR-21 gas turbines. The alternator is extremely compact thanks to its advanced cooling system and is designed to withstand the high levels of harmonics typical of an electrical propulsion

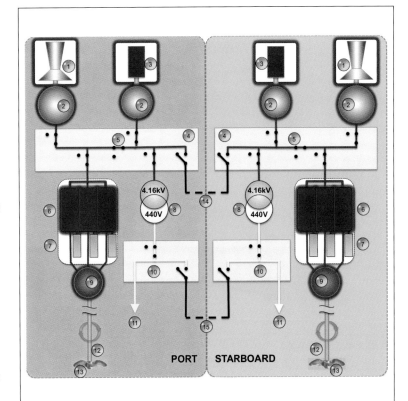

1 Gas turbine.
2 Alternator.
3 Diesel.
4 4.16kV switchboard.
5 Busbar tie.
6 Converter.
7 Dynamic breaking resistors.
8 Ship's service transformer 2.5MVA.
9 Propulsion motor.
10 440V switchboard.
11 Ship's service supply 440V, three-phase, 60Hz.
12 Propeller shaft.
13 Propeller.
14 4.16kV interconnector.
15 440V interconnector.

ABOVE Integrated electrical propulsion system single line diagram showing the 'twin-island' full-power configuration (4.16kV filters omitted for simplicity). *(Author from GE Energy information)*

BELOW Cutaway diagram of a WR-21 advance cycle gas turbine with alternator attached. *(Rolls-Royce)*

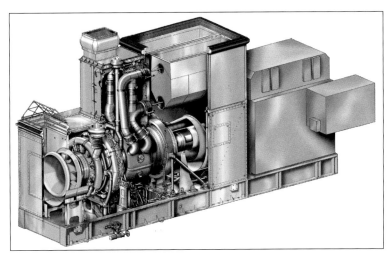

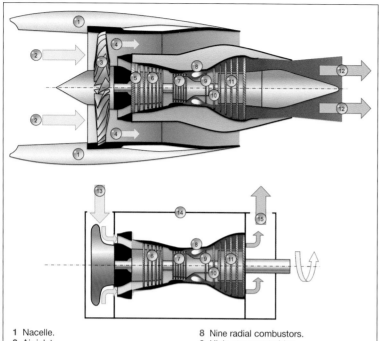

1 Nacelle.
2 Air inlet.
3 Turbofan.
4 Bypass air.
5 Two-stage low-pressure compressor.
6 Six-stage intermediate-pressure compressor.
7 Six-stage high-pressure compressor.
8 Nine radial combustors.
9 High-pressure turbine.
10 Intermediate-pressure turbine.
11 Five-stage power turbine.
12 Exhaust thrust.
13 Air inlet (down-take).
14 Turbine enclosure.
15 Exhaust (up-take).

ABOVE Marine gas turbine (bottom) derived from aero-engine (top). *(Author from Rolls-Royce information)*

system. The WR-21 and alternator are mounted on a common base plate that is, in turn, resiliently mounted to the ship to mute the transmission of any vibration to the ship's hull. All aspects of the GTAs are regulated by a full authority digital engine control system.

The WR-21 is a marine gas turbine derived from an aero-engine but contained in a gastight and watertight enclosure that is force-ventilated. Benefiting greatly from the advanced aero-engine technology, the high-pressure turbine blades are manufactured to withstand the extraordinary demands placed upon them by the high speed of rotation of the turbine and the extremely hot exhaust gases. Each blade is made from a single crystal of a special alloy. The crystal is formed in a vacuum furnace by a technique that ensures that, as it grows, it incorporates a complex series of air passages used in operation to cool the blade. Incredibly accurate laser drilling creates external cooling holes before a thermal barrier coating is applied. This coating surpasses the performance of the tiles coating the Space Shuttle and can operate in gas temperatures that not only exceed the melting point of the blade's alloy but does so by more than 400°C.

The WR-21 is the world's first advanced cycle gas turbine with both intercooled and recuperated cycles that contribute to its exceptional power efficiency and fuel economy. Both techniques employ counterflow plate-fin heat exchangers to reuse heat that would otherwise be wasted.

All gases increase in temperature if their pressure is increased, so air leaving the intermediate-pressure compressor is hotter than input air. The intercooler reduces the temperature of the air leaving the compressor, so reducing the power required to compress the air in the second stage (high-pressure) compressor. The intercooler also reduces the discharge temperature of the high-pressure compressor, thereby enhancing the performance of the next energy-saving cycle, the recuperator.

The low temperature exhaust gases leaving the third and final turbine of the engine enter the recuperator where they are used to preheat the compressed air before it enters the combustor. The recuperator's operation is enhanced by hydraulically actuated variable area nozzles that allow it to be used to full effect. The recuperator

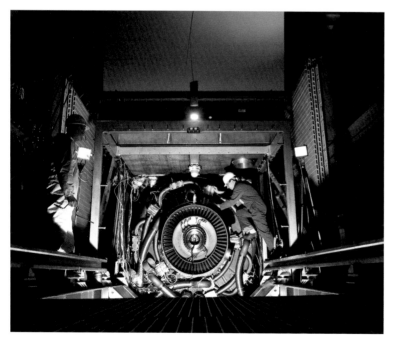

LEFT Maintenance of a WR-21 marine gas turbine within its enclosure. *(Rolls-Royce)*

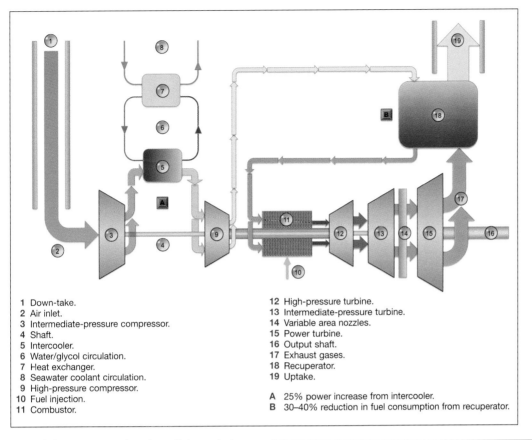

LEFT Schematic of WR-21 intercooled and recuperated marine gas turbine. *(Author from Rolls-Royce information)*

1 Down-take.
2 Air inlet.
3 Intermediate-pressure compressor.
4 Shaft.
5 Intercooler.
6 Water/glycol circulation.
7 Heat exchanger.
8 Seawater coolant circulation.
9 High-pressure compressor.
10 Fuel injection.
11 Combustor.

12 High-pressure turbine.
13 Intermediate-pressure turbine.
14 Variable area nozzles.
15 Power turbine.
16 Output shaft.
17 Exhaust gases.
18 Recuperator.
19 Uptake.

A 25% power increase from intercooler.
B 30–40% reduction in fuel consumption from recuperator.

not only improves combustion efficiency but also lowers the exhaust gas temperature as it leaves the up-take, so reducing the infrared signature of the warship.

The intercooled and recuperated cycles for the WR-21 marine gas turbines required the development of a combustion system that differs significantly from those of a conventional gas turbine. The combustor features a reflex airspray burner method of fuel injection. This achieves a controlled mixing of fuel and air, allowing the air-fuel ratio to be higher (lean burn) while maintaining adequate flame stability. This is an important factor in reducing visible smoke.

Two diesel alternators provide a secondary source of 4.16kV electrical power and power the ship's services when in harbour. As with the GTAs, each diesel engine and its alternator is attached to a base plate that is, in turn, resiliently mounted on the ship's structure. Each diesel alternator is contained in an acoustic enclosure. The diesel engine speed sets the output frequency of the alternator and is controlled by an automatic voltage regulator. A second regulator, located within the switchboard enclosure, controls its output voltage.

Gas turbine alternator key characteristics	
Power (gas turbine/alternator)	25MW/21.6MWe (4.16kV, 0.9 power factor lag)
Specific fuel consumption	about 0.86m³/kWh
Dimensions (L x W x H)	8m x 3.56m x 1.13m
Weight main module wet	45,974kg
Weight overall dry	49,693kg
Intermediate compressor	Six-stage with intercooler
High-pressure compressor	Six-stage with exhaust heat recuperator
Combustor	Nine radial combustors
High-pressure turbine	Single-stage 8,100rpm (135 rev/sec)
Intermediate-pressure turbine	Single-stage 6,200rpm (103 rev/sec)
Power turbine	Five-stage 3,600rpm (60 rev/sec)

Diesel alternator key characteristics	
Power (engine/alternator)	2.0MW/1.73MWe (4.16kV, 0.9 power factor lag)
Fuel	Diesel or light fuel oil
Bore/stroke	200mm/240mm
Weight	27,000kg
Speed	1,500rpm (25 rev/sec)
Prime running power continuous operation (24hr average, 90% load) at 60Hz, 2.0MWe.	
Limited time power (maximum continuous is 300hr, maximum 500hr/year) at 60Hz, 2.2MWe.	

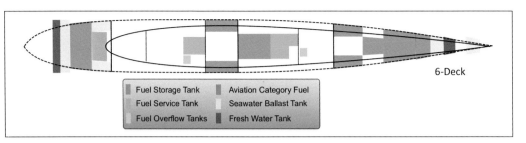

Fuel Storage Tank	Aviation Category Fuel
Fuel Service Tank	Seawater Ballast Tank
Fuel Overflow Tanks	Fresh Water Tank

6-Deck

ABOVE The diesel alternator enclosure. *(Crown Copyright, 2012 HMS Defender)*

BELOW The 20MW advanced induction motor. *(Crown Copyright, 2012 HMS Defender)*

Diesel fuel for the prime movers is held in a number of tanks low in the hull. Fuel for the engines is drawn from service tanks that are regularly refilled from the storage tanks. In order to reduce marine growth in the tanks, the diesel fuel stripping system removes water, residues and contaminates from the fuel. Before use, the fuel is filtered to remove any further traces of contaminant. The balance of the ship's weight changes as fuel (and, to a lesser extent, stores) are embarked and expended, To maintain ship trim and stability, fuel is pumped between the storage tanks and in addition five seawater ballast tanks have their contents adjusted to compensate for weight changes. The ships also have solid ballast in the lowest part of the hull, but this is only changed during refits when the permanent equipment is altered. Solid ballast amounts to less than 1% of the ship's displacement.

In order to drive the ship's propellers, the reversible AIMs have to operate at relatively low speed and high torque. To meet the space constraints of a warship they must also have a very high power-density. This has been achieved without any penalties in performance by optimising the electro-magnetic design, giving a high air gap shear stress of $100kN/m^2$. This measure of power-density is more than seven times that of a standard large industrial induction motor and approaching that of the permanent magnet synchronous motor. The output power of 20MW can thus be achieved with a motor of only 100 tonnes and a volume of $36m^3$.

Induction motors are inherently robust compared with other rotating electrical machines. The strength of the AIM is further enhanced by constructing the rotor, its most vulnerable part, from simple solid copper conductors contained in slots within an iron core and without electrical insulation. The converter arrangement allows for great flexibility in operation and facilitates this optimum electro-magnetic design. This, in turn, allows a larger air gap between the stator and rotor, enhancing its capability to withstand shock. The AIM is consequently qualified to exacting MoD shock standards.

The AIMs are each cooled by four variable-speed fans that circulate air within the motor. The construction of both stator and rotor incorporates radial ventilation ducts known as 'pin-vents' that provide an efficient way of removing heat from the windings. The circulating air is cooled by the heat exchangers of the converter seawater cooling system.

RIGHT Cutaway of an advanced induction motor.
(GE Energy)

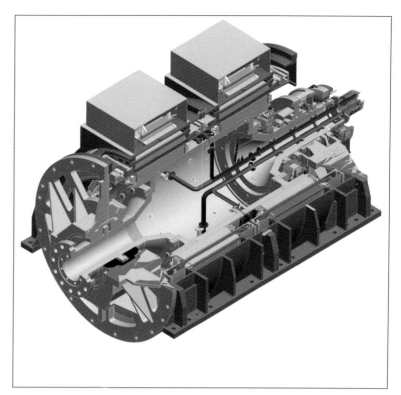

RIGHT Cutaway of an advanced induction motor.
(GE Energy)

The AIMs are directly coupled to the propeller shafts, obviating the need for traditional gearboxes or controllable pitch propeller systems. Each motor can run on 5, 10 or 15 phases depending on converter channel availability and whether or not the priority is low noise signature or high efficiency. Low radiated noise signature (quiet mode operation) demands all phases, while high efficiency demands the minimum number of phases for the output power required.

The Type 45 destroyer is notable for the first implementation of a voltage source main propulsion converter in a warship. Each converter, fed directly from their respective 4.16kV switchboard, controls the speed and power of an AIM. The converter varies the frequency of the motor's supply and hence the motor's rotational speed. The converters provide variable frequency supplies in two stages. First they change the 60Hz, 4.16kV AC to DC by means of a thyristor rectifier. An insulated gate bipolar transistor inverter then constructs the correct waveform using pulse-width modulation in order to drive the motor at the correct speed. The converters have three separately mounted channels, each driving five phases of its associated AIM. When the ship is not powered, the converter's air-cooled dynamic braking resistors absorb power from propulsion motors. This enables the propeller shaft to rapidly reduce its speed and then to reverse its direction of rotation. This contributes significantly to the superior stopping capability of Type 45 destroyers.

The converters contain full authority digital engine controllers that considerably enhance the stability of the system by, among other features, maintaining propulsion power within the available generation capacity.

Both the 4.16kV converters and non-linear 440V loads produce waveform distortion of the power supply by generating additional high-frequency components. Harmonic filters at both voltages are connected to the switchboards to reduce this distortion and the consequent heating effects in the alternators. The 440V filters

ABOVE VDM25000 converter. *(GE Energy)*

LEFT High-voltage harmonic filter. *(GE Energy)*

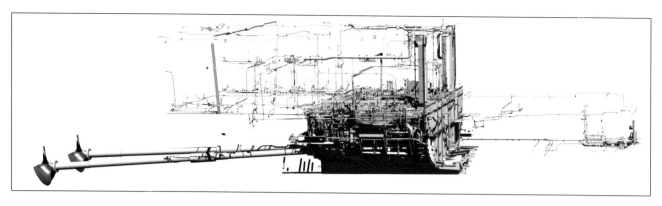

ABOVE Artist's impression of main propulsion system. (Alex Pang)

are active filters that can also compensate for harmonics generated by the 440V system itself.

The EPMS responds to commands from the platform management system (PMS) and automatically reconfigures the IEPS. For example, demands for changes in ship's speed input into the PMS will result in the EPMS adjusting the converter frequency to change the motor speed and, consequently, the propeller speed. Other automatic control functions of the EPMS are ensuring that the running alternators are balanced, maintaining the system voltages and synchronising alternators that are to be connected. If there is a warning that an alternator may fail then it can automatically start prime movers in anticipation of the emergency.

Main propeller shafting

The immense power and torque of the propulsion system is transmitted from each AIM to the relevant propeller by a main propulsion shaft that is connected to the AIM by means of a flange. The AIM, shaft and propeller consequently all rotate at the same speed but rotate in opposite directions. The shafts are tubular, over 500mm in diameter, with a wall thickness of over 40mm within the ship, increasing to over 50mm outboard. The port shaft, driven from the forward AIM, is 60m long whereas the starboard shaft, driven by the aft AIM is almost 40m long. Each passes through a thrust block close to the motor. This transmits the thrust from the propeller to the ship's structure. The eight double-tilting bearings of the thrust blocks are immersed in oil lubricant.

Inboard there are three plummer blocks to support the port shaft but only a single plummer block for the shorter starboard shaft. Like the thrust blocks, their bearings are immersed in lubricant. Low-pressure seawater circulating in cooling coils submerged in their lubricant removes heat from both types of block.

Each shaft passes through the hull at a stern tube gland that is designed to limit any ingress of water to 0.6m³/day. An inflatable seal is incorporated in the stern gland and this allows maintenance to be carried out without the expense of docking the ship.

The shafts are also each fitted with a hydraulically operated propeller shaft brake that can be activated in an extreme emergency to stop the shaft in a few seconds. For shaft maintenance shaft locking gear stops the unpowered shaft from rotating, whereas the shaft turning gear allows it to be slowly rotated for maintenance purposes.

The five-bladed 4.85m-diameter nickel–aluminium–bronze propellers have a fixed pitch. The propellers comprise a hollow hub with blades bolted to it from the inside using only hand tools. Such an adjustable bolted propeller is lighter than a tradition monobloc propeller (one cast as a single unit). A bolted propeller offers fast and simple installation and replacement of blades without the need to enter a dry dock. Higher-quality blade machining and easier manufacturing is possible with individual blades compared to a monobloc propeller.

BELOW Schematic of starboard main shafting. (Author from BAE Systems information)

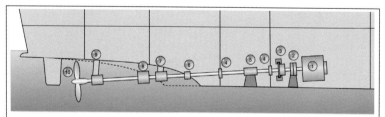

1 Advanced propulsion motor.	6 Stern tube gland.
2 Thrust block.	7 Intermediate 'A' bracket.
3 Shaft brake.	8 Muff coupling.
4 Bulkhead gland.	9 Main 'A' bracket.
5 Plummer block.	10 Adjustable blade propeller.

Stabilisers and steering gear

The electro-hydraulic active fin stabilising system is used to reduce the warship's roll motion in heavy weather. Stabilisation creates a more comfortable working environment for the ship's company so increases their effectiveness. It also makes the ship more effective as a weapons platform and increases the helicopter's operating envelope to higher sea states. The system has two streamlined fins protruding from the ship's hull towards the stern. These are automatically rotated so as to produce hydrodynamic forces in opposition to the hull's roll motion, so reducing the rolling.

The actuated steering gear consists of two electro-hydraulically operated rudders. In normal operation the ship's course can be automatically set using an autopilot. So, for instance, the ship can follow a pre-selected route plotted on the electronic chart, display and information system. As might be expected for such an important system, there are fallback and backup configurations to ensure that steerage may be achieved provided that at least one rudder is functional. In an emergency the rudders may be operated using an emergency hand-pump and wheel located adjacent to the steering gear.

440V AC electrical distribution

The port and starboard 4.16kV switchboards are each connected to a ship's service transformer that provides 440V AC electrical power. Each of the 440V switchboards then distributes 400V, three-phase, 60Hz AC power to equipment throughout the ship. The breakers in the 440V switchboards are air circuit breakers or, for consumer loads, moulded-case circuit breakers. Under peacetime low-load conditions the switchboards can be interconnected and all 440V power drawn from a single transformer.

Normally the forward (starboard) and aft 440V switchboards each supply power to:

- Two air conditioning compressors.
- A converter seawater pump.
- Two high-pressure seawater system pumps.

ABOVE HMS *Daring* at sea in a swell. *(Crown Copyright, 2012 LA(Phot) Caroline (Caz) Davies)*

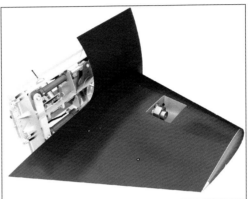

LEFT Starboard stabilising fin from aft. *(Rolls-Royce)*

LEFT Twin-rudder actuated steering gear. *(Rolls-Royce)*

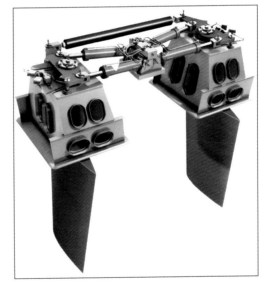

BELOW Steering electro-hydraulic actuators in HMS *Defender*'s steering gear compartment. *(Crown Copyright, 2012 HMS Defender)*

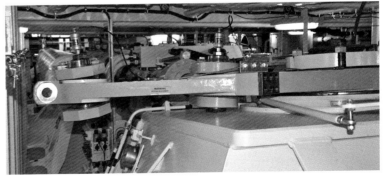

- A calorifier.
- Six (forward switchboard) or seven (aft switchboard) electrical distribution centres.

Each also has a damage control connection and a link to the emergency switchboard.

Apart from the large power loads directly provided from the switchboards, most equipment is supplied from one of the electrical distribution centres located throughout the ship. The majority of ship's equipment is 440V but the centres also incorporate:

- Transformers to supply 115V, single-phase, 60Hz (domestic) equipment.
- Inverters to supply 400Hz equipment.
- Transformer rectifier units to supply 24V DC equipment.

If power to either the port (aft) or starboard switchboards fails then its electrical distribution centres are connected to the other switchboard so that supplies are maintained. This transition is achieved rapidly by automatic changeover switches, ensuring the almost seamless recovery of 440V and 115V supplies. There is the potential for overloading the healthy switchboard when it is connected to all 13 electrical distribution centres. To prevent this, each centre is equipped with connections to 440V equipment and 115V transformers that may be disconnected (shed) automatically by the electrical power control and management system. However, provided there is sufficient capacity, the failed switchboard's calorifier may then be manually connected to the healthy switchboard.

There is a third (emergency) switchboard that is normally supplied by the starboard 440V switchboard through an automatic change-over switch. The switch immediately changes the supply to the port 440V switchboard should the forward switchboard lose power. The emergency switchboard supplies power to vital equipment (that required for watertight integrity and life-saving) and to essential equipment (that necessary for immediate operational functions and steerage of the ship). In the event of total power failure of the 4.16kV system an emergency diesel generator connected to the emergency switchboard provides power to vital and essential equipment. This generator has its own ready-use fuel supply for a few hours' operation.

Machinery spaces

The large port and starboard GTAs are sited in the forward gas turbine room and the aft gas turbine room respectively. To accommodate the GTAs, these rooms are two decks high, extending from 5-Deck to the deckhead of 4-Deck. They occupy the whole width and length of the section on these decks. The rooms also contain an AIM and a great deal of ancillary equipment. The shaft from the aft motor drives the starboard propeller. The forward motor drives the port propeller through a long shaft that also passes through the aft gas turbine room. The space taken up by this shaft means that the aft diesel alternator has to be accommodated in the aft

BELOW **Single line diagram of the 440V AC distribution system in seagoing line-up with both gas turbine alternators on-line (440V filters and shore supply connections omitted for simplicity).** *(Author from GE Energy information)*

PORT   **STARBOARD**

1 4.16kV supply.
2 Ship's service transformer 2.5MVA.
3 Switchboard 440V, three-phase, 60Hz.
4 Interconnector.
5 Normal/alternative supply to electrical distribution centres.
6 Emergency 440V switchboard.
7 Large loads.
8 Damage control connection.
9 Distribution panels.
10 Steering motors (port and starboard).
11 Emergency diesel alternator 250kW.
12 High-pressure air compressor No 3.

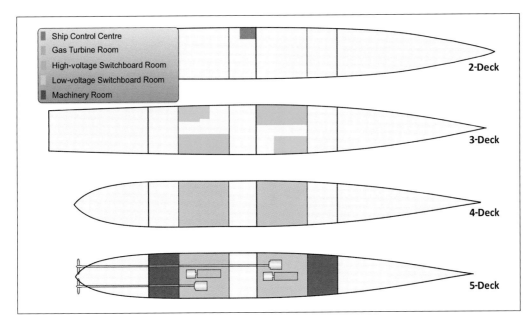

Legend:
- Ship Control Centre
- Gas Turbine Room
- High-voltage Switchboard Room
- Low-voltage Switchboard Room
- Machinery Room

2-Deck

3-Deck

4-Deck

5-Deck

LEFT Diagram of machinery spaces. *(Author from BAE Systems information)*

BELOW High-voltage switchboard in HMS *Defender*'s high-voltage equipment room. *(Crown Copyright, 2012 HMS Defender)*

BOTTOM HMS *Defender*'s low-voltage equipment room. *(Crown Copyright, 2012 HMS Defender)*

machinery room, whereas the forward diesel alternator is accommodated in the forward gas turbine room.

On 3-Deck above the aft gas turbine rooms are the aft high-voltage and aft low-voltage equipment rooms. The former contains a 4.16kV switchboard, a 4.16kV harmonic filter, an automatic voltage regulator and the three propulsion converters related to the GTA on the deck below. In addition, the compartment contains the automatic voltage regulators for the aft diesel alternator, a battery cubicle and its battery charger.

The low-voltage equipment room contains a 440V switchboard, a 440V harmonic filter, a 4.16kV/440V transformer and an uninterruptible power supply for essential 440V equipment. The forward high-voltage switchboard room and low-voltage switchboard rooms are located above the forward gas turbine room but are mirror images of their aft equivalents.

The exhaust gases from the forward gas turbine and diesel engine pass through an

up-take on the ship's centreline, through the funnel, and leave the superstructure at 04-Deck level. The aft gas turbine up-take travels up under the LRR mast before bending aft and

JACKSPEAK

Unlike the relatively roomy IEPS machinery spaces, older ships, especially those with steam systems, had machinery spaces that were a tangle of pipework. Such pipework was often described as a 'snakes' wedding' – a term that is now generally applied to a particularly confused and complex situation.

joining the aft diesel engine up-take to emerge on 04-Deck behind the radar's mast. All NATO warships have means of cooling their exhaust gases to reduce the ships' infrared signature, usually by entrainment of cool air through several annular vents within the upper levels of the up-take. The down-takes supplying air to ventilate the gas turbine rooms and for their gas turbines are forward of the up-takes. They draw in air through filters from partially enclosed spaces in order to reduce the ingress of water. As down-takes are much simpler in construction than the up-takes they are designed to be the removal and shipping routes for the gas turbine's modules should these require replacement.

ABOVE Forward and aft up-take for exhaust gases from gas turbines and diesel engines. *(Crown Copyright, 2011 LA(Phot) Ben Sutton)*

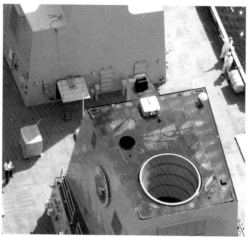

RIGHT Detail of forward up-takes showing the large gas turbine and the smaller diesel up-take. *(Alan Paxton)*

Ship control centre (SCC) and platform management system (PMS)

Located on 2-Deck, between the forward and aft machinery sections, the SCC is the primary location for the control of all aspects of the ship's propulsion system and marine systems. When at action stations it is here that the marine engineering team manages those functions that enable the ship to move, float and provide a viable environment for the ship's personnel. It is also the centre for coordinating damage control actions.

The system that facilitates the marine engineers' tasks is the PMS. This concentrates into a single entity all the destroyer's support services and, furthermore, integrates systems that contribute to the vessel's mobility and sustainability. It allows operators to access, monitor and control all of these functions from a single fixed workstation. All its workstations are capable of running the full functions of machinery control and surveillance, damage surveillance and control and platform management support services. It automates many of the machinery and auxiliary control processes, thereby greatly simplifying or completely relieving the operator of mundane and regular tasks. The programmable logic controllers of the machinery control and surveillance system are capable of automatically performing complicated machinery reconfigurations – for example, allowing the operator to start a GTA with just one click.

RIGHT Detail of the two aft down-take filters (with ventilation jalousie beneath the far, starboard, filter). *(Airfix)*

The fixed workstations each have two displays (side by side), two tracker-balls (one for each display) and a keyboard. The workstation used by the Marine Engineering Officer of the Watch also has propulsion speed control levers similar to those on the bridge. However, any workstation may control this function through the virtual levers on their display. From any workstation, operators can control and monitor the ship's propulsion and service equipment at the click of a mouse through 450 active graphic screens that have been specially designed for intuitive operation. The operators can select, or be allocated, particular systems to monitor

and control. These systems and their status are displayed on the left-hand display, with the right-hand display showing the schematic for the selected system. The schematic can be used to control the displayed system – for instance, to start or stop pumps or vary pressures.

In addition to the five fixed workstations in the SCC there are a further seven similar, dual-display, fixed workstations throughout the ship, and five portable single-display rugged laptop workstations that can be plugged into one of 20 dedicated ship-wide locations. These portable workstations can also connect to the PMS anywhere in the ship where there is Ethernet

ABOVE LEFT Ship control centre at action stations on HMS *Diamond*. *(Crown Copyright, 2013 PO(Phot) Paul Punter)*

ABOVE HMS *Diamond*'s Marine Engineering Officer of the Watch at ship control centre workstation with engine control levers. *(Crown Copyright , 2011 PO(Phot) Paul Punter)*

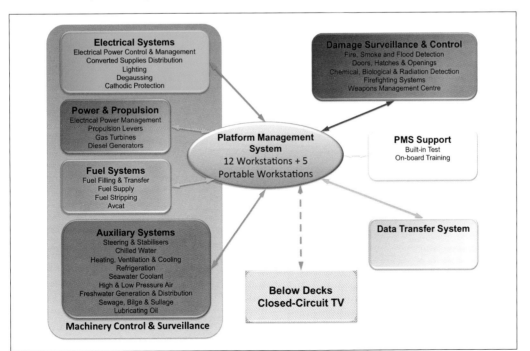

LEFT Schematic of ship's systems integrated, monitored and controlled by the platform management system. *(Author from BAE Systems information)*

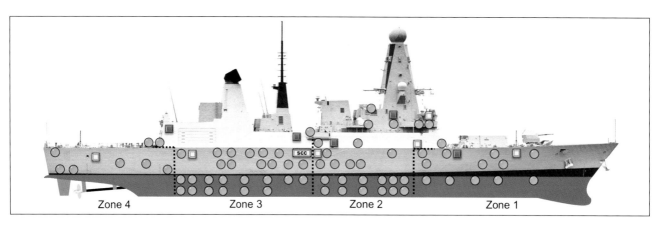

| Zone 4 | Zone 3 | Zone 2 | Zone 1 |

connectivity. Consequently there are almost a hundred points where normal maintenance or damage control stations can be established.

The PMS includes built-in test and fault diagnosis so that failures can be detected and rectified speedily. It also provides a similar function for the propulsion machinery through its condition-based monitoring. This monitoring system records machinery statistics (*eg* running hours), events, performance changes and data for analysis (such as exhaust gas temperature). It allows preventive maintenance and machinery changes to be accurately scheduled. Also built into the system is a scenario-based training facility to allow operators to continue to improve their performance.

Thanks to a high degree of flexibility and redundancy, if a fault occurs (or if action damage has been sustained) the PMS automatically reconfigures systems so that they can continue

to operate. The damage surveillance and control system provides the operator with an automated picture of any damage sustained and advises on additional manual intervention needed to control floods, fires and system outages. It can perform a recovery from a total ship electrical power failure without the need for intervention by a human operator. One of the damage control functions that it performs is the automatic shedding of non-essential power supplies if there is damage to the ship's electrical power distribution system. It thereby ensures that, in the event of a partial power failure, key combat and marine systems have priority for power over domestic requirements.

The PMS's high degree of automation and the convenient display of detailed information has been a factor in the reduction of ship's staff needed to operate the propulsion and other marine systems. Workload has been further reduced by use of remote monitoring of an increased number of marine systems sensors and the use of closed-circuit television (CCTV) cameras. These have dramatically reduced the need for watch-keepers to patrol the machinery spaces and take regular readings.

On-board degaussing (OBDG) system

Magnetic fields produced by ships may trigger mines. To reduce the magnetic signature of the ship, an OBDG system is fitted to counteract both the ship's permanent magnetic field and those effects induced by the Earth's magnetic field. The latter varies with the geographic location and heading of the ship. The system produces compensating magnetic fields by passing electrical currents through

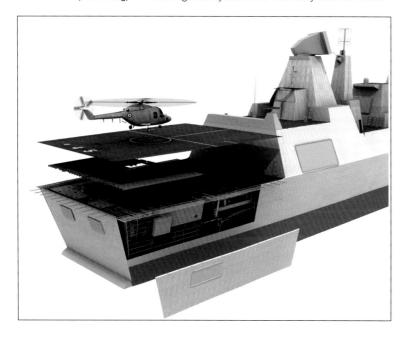

19 coils within the ship's hull. The current to the coils is varied to ensure that the ship's magnetic signature is reduced to an acceptable level. A coil drive unit, called a bi-polar amplifier unit, provides the power supply to each coil. The system is a semi-distributed one, with the coil drive units grouped together at three locations within the ship. This arrangement reduces power usage, weight, coil length and overall cost when compared to a distributed system where the coil drive units are located with each coil. The system is fully automatic, with the coil currents regulated by a signature management controller. In the event of the loss of a coil, special survivability algorithms in the control software adjust the currents in the remaining coils to minimise the ship's magnetic signature.

Boat bays and Pacific 24 rigid inflatable boat (RIB)

On either side of the hangar is a boat bay. Each is two decks high in order to accommodate a ship's sea boat, the Pacific 24 RIB, and its specialist launch and recovery davit system. RIBs are fast service boats that allow warships to conduct a variety of patrol and boarding operations. Each boat requires a crew of two, who occupy the helm position aft, behind the engine; forward is removable modular seating for up to six additional occupants. The Pacific 24 is based on a hull-form already used by the RN and that has proven to have exceptional sea-keeping characteristics and load-carrying capability. The hull is made from epoxy reinforced with carbon and Kevlar fibre. The boat is fitted with modern communications and other equipment necessary to support the boat's principal roles as well as safety equipment such as an aft 'A' frame with a capsize reversal system.

In each bay, the RIB is supported on a cradle with an easy-chock release mechanism and four grab arms. Deployment (and subsequent recovery) of the boat can be controlled remotely using an electro-hydraulic system, although there is also a manual emergency backup system. To launch the boat, the chocks are automatically withdrawn and the guardrails automatically lowered. The four-tined grab mechanism moves outboard

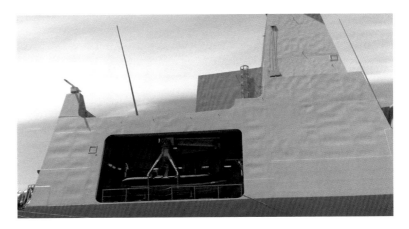

on a gantry until the boat is suspended over the sea. The bespoke boat davit system lowers the boat, complete with full crew, to the sea's surface. The davit incorporates a special anti-pendulation device and a wave compensation facility to optimise the safety and control of the

TOP Starboard boat bay open to show Pacific 24 rigid inflatable boat suspended from davit. *(Pellegrini)*

ABOVE HMS *Daring*'s Pacific 24 rigid inflatable boat operating in the waters of the Middle East. *(Crown Copyright, 2013 LA(Phot) Dave Jenkins)*

LEFT Pacific 24 rigid inflatable boat being deployed by HMS *Diamond*. *(Crown Copyright, 2010 LA(Phot) Gary Weatherston)*

boat during launch and recovery. The RIB's engine has a dry running ability that allows engines to be started on davits before it enters the water.

Each boat bay has a twin-movement closure, 9m long by 4.25m high, that provides protection from the elements and reduces the ship's radar cross-section. The closures have louvres to provide ventilation to the boat bays.

Pacific 24 rigid inflatable boat	
Overall length	7.8m
Overall beam	2.6m
Draught	0.54m approx
Height (excluding antennas)	2.3m
Hosting weight	2,500kg
Fuel	165 litres
Typical range at 56km/h (30 knots)	280km (150NM)
Engine	6-cylinder Yanmar 6LYA-STP
Water-jet	Hamilton HJ 241
Speed	>72km/h (39 knots)

The hangar

The two-deck-high hangar provides a space protected from the weather where the ship's embarked helicopter may be stored and maintained. The helicopter is not only a useful transport system, but augments the warship's sensor suite and provides a means of rapidly delivering weapons to locations that cannot be reached by the ship itself.

On entering service, the Type 45 destroyers each carried a single Lynx helicopter. However, the hangar was designed to accommodate two Lynx helicopters or, alternatively, an embarked Merlin helicopter. To fit into the hangar, the rotors of both Lynx and Merlin helicopters have to be stowed. The tail sections of both helicopters can be folded forward alongside their fuselage to reduce their overall length when in the hangar. This is essential to accommodate the Merlin. The hangar and nearby air weapons magazine can cater for spares and stores for items for both helicopters, such as sonobuoys for the Merlin's anti-submarine warfare (ASW) tasks.

Trials undertaken by HMS *Dauntless* demonstrated that two Lynx helicopters could be stowed in a Type 45 hangar. After the first Lynx lands there is a period when the flight deck is 'blacked' (unavailable for landing), because only one Lynx at a time can be accommodated on the flight deck. Until the first helicopter is moved to the hangar there would be difficulties if the airborne helicopter developed a problem and could not be diverted to another platform. For this reason, multi-aircraft operations from a single deck-spot are challenging and require a highly efficient flight-deck crew who can rapidly move the helicopter to the hangar. Once the first Lynx is in the hangar, the second can land.

The hangar is equipped with a gantry crane that can lift the rotor assembly from both the Lynx and Merlin helicopters for maintenance

BELOW Lynx helicopter with folded rotors on the MANTIS mobile helicopter handling equipment secured in the hangar of HMS *Diamond*. *(Daniel Ferro)*

BELOW RIGHT Air mechanics fold the rotors of a Lynx HMA Mk8 SRU helicopter. *(Crown Copyright, 2011)*

and enable other maintenance tasks to be readily performed. It is an X–Y crane, with a safe working load of 1.5 tonnes, that can move fore and aft as well as athwartships. The hangar incorporates a mezzanine deck at 01-Deck level that holds, among other equipment, the main rotor store.

The helicopter maintainers have MANTIS mobile helicopter handling equipment to move helicopters between the flight deck and the hangar and to steer them within the hangar. It is capable of manoeuvring the 13-tonne Merlin helicopter even when the ship is moving violently in significant sea states.

In the extreme aft starboard side of the superstructure is the Flight-Deck Officer's caboose. This small compartment has a large window (fitted with a wiper to remove rain or spray) that gives an excellent view of the flight deck. The position is equipped with a radar display fed from the rear Type 1047 navigation radar (sited immediately above on the hangar roof) and requisite

communications equipment. It is from here that the launch and recovery of helicopters, and flight-deck operations is controlled.

As well as two doors that lead from the superstructure to the flight deck, the large two-deck-high aluminium hangar closure connects

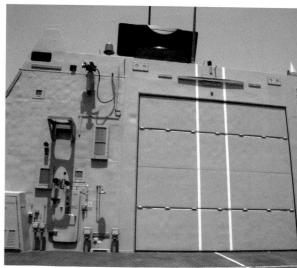

ABOVE **Partially open hangar closure from the flight deck – to starboard is the window of the Flight-Deck Officer's caboose.** *(Daniel Ferro)*

ABOVE RIGHT **Four-blade hangar closure.** *(Daniel Ferro)*

BELOW **HMS *Daring*'s flight deck.** *(Crown Copyright, 2008 LA(Phot) Del Trotter)*

the hangar and the flight deck. Stores can be easily brought on board to the flight deck from the dockside; the hangar closure acts as a useful route to rapidly move the stores under cover into the hangar until they can be moved through the ship to storage compartments.

The hangar closure provides a clear hangar opening of 6.4m wide by 5.8m high, and is made of four aluminium sections called blades. Its lightweight construction means that it is easy and quiet to operate yet shockproof, corrosion-proof and able to withstand wind and bad weather. It is electrically operated and is able to go from fully open to fully shut (or vice versa) in 60 seconds under normal conditions. The door can be stopped and remain safely fixed at any position between fully closed and fully open. Like the ship's superstructure, the hangar closure is sloped at 6° off the vertical for radar cross-section reduction purposes. In the case of a flight-deck fire the closure will protect the hangar and any stowed helicopter from fire and smoke. Fire protection is achieved by the high thermal insulation of the blades and the provision of an intumescent fire protection strip beneath the lowest blade. When heated this swells to prevent flames reaching the hangar.

The flight deck

HMS *Daring*'s flight deck covers an area greater than a doubles tennis court. It can accommodate Lynx helicopters, the much larger Merlin helicopters or even the twin-rotor Chinook helicopter. At just under 30m long, its length is determined by the diameter of the Chinook's rotors plus a safe clearance to the superstructure, allowing for room to manoeuvre when landing on a moving deck in bad weather. This flight deck is almost double the area of that of the Batch I Type 42 destroyers. It is even about 25% longer than the ASW Type 23 (*Duke Class*) frigates' flight decks that were designed to operate Merlin helicopters.

While the flight deck is intended for helicopter operations, the space is invaluable for other purposes, especially when alongside. At the forward end of the flight deck, port and starboard, are a set of bollards and a fairlead to secure the ship alongside, and a pair of 24-person life rafts. The sides of the flight deck, from the superstructure aft about 8m, have railings, but the remainder of the flight deck has stanchions to support netting. The stanchions also support long strips of lighting that help define the deck-edge for helicopter operations. When a helicopter is landing obstructions

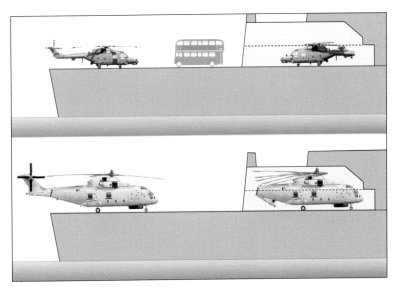

must be cleared, so the stanchions and their netting are dropped outboard to the horizontal position. The deck-edge lights, previously shining in towards the deck, now face upwards, providing firm positional cues for the pilot. These lights provide just some of the lighting to

ABOVE The flight deck and hangar showing Lynx and Merlin helicopter outlines (and London Routemaster bus for comparison). *(Author/ AgustaWestland)*

LEFT Flight deck showing the rotor span of Lynx (red), Merlin (yellow) and twin-rotor Chinook (blue) helicopters. *(Author/ AgustaWestland)*

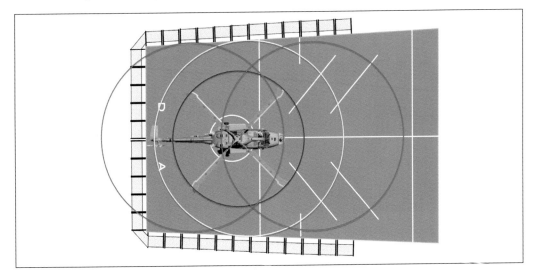

FAR LEFT Port flight-deck bollard and fairlead with (against superstructure) two 24-person life rafts, railings and the locker for defuelling equipment. *(Airfix)*

LEFT Detail of the flight-deck stanchions and netting. *(Crown Copyright, 2012 LA(Phot) Chris Mumby)*

The enclosed quarterdeck

Beneath the flight deck is the enclosed quarterdeck. Traditionally the quarterdeck has had large openings so that mooring lines and towed underwater sensors can be readily deployed. Like the enclosed forecastle, the weather protection of the enclosed quarterdeck provides a better working environment than an open foredeck, decreases degradation of the equipment and reduces the warship's radar cross-section.

The enclosed quarterdeck has five-tonne mooring capstans and fairleads in the transom, as well as bollards (used primarily to make the ship fast when alongside). In addition, there is the equipment and working space necessary to undertake the emergency towing of other ships.

The fairleads, two transom closures and

outline the ship's structure (there are additional lights on the superstructure and hull) and key flight-deck positions. They form part of the helicopter visual approach system that includes an advanced stabilised glide slope indicator for the approaching helicopter, line-up lights, a stabilised horizon reference system, a pilot information display and a wave-off light.

ABOVE LEFT HMS *Defender*'s enclosed quarterdeck transom showing mooring capstan and transom closures. *(Crown Copyright, 2012 HMS* Defender*)*

ABOVE HMS *Daring*'s transom showing two large fairleads, two transom doors and the port divers' door. *(Steve Wagstaff)*

LEFT Transom closures seen from the enclosed quarterdeck. *(Crown Copyright, 2012 HMS* Defender*)*

divers' door can be clearly identified from outside the ship. The transom closures are retained by ten clips but can be opened by a single handle and secured partially or fully against the hull. Their movement is assisted by an electro-hydraulic system operating a fail-safe rack and pinion mechanism, which can, however, also be locked manually. The transom closures are of a composite structure with inbuilt ventilation louvres. The divers' doors and seamanship doors are of a similar construction to those of the enclosed foredeck.

High-pressure seawater (HPSW) and other seawater systems

The HPSW system is supplied with seawater by eight electrically driven centrifugal pumps that operate at constant speed and discharge 250m³/h at 760kPa. The system's horizontal ring main is maintained at 550kPa and provides water for firefighting. It is the source of seawater for water spray systems, magazine spray systems, foam sprays, and fire hydrants. The HPSW also provides water for the pre-wetting system and for cooling for main machinery, steering gear and the Phalanx CIWS. Filling and emptying of the MFS dome is a further function of the HPSW system.

Two emergency fire pumps can supplement the seawater supply to the ring main in an emergency. These diesel-driven HPSW pumps can deliver 100m³/hr at 700kPa. They have a suction lift of 3.5m for pumping out spaces flooded by damage or by water used for firefighting.

A second seawater system, operating at a similar high pressure, is the water auxiliary cooling system that is used to cool the propulsion motors, propulsion converters and 440V electrical filters. Should the water auxiliary cooling system fail, then the equipment that it normally supplies can be cooled by the HPSW.

Apart from the HPSW system there are two low-pressure cooling systems: the low-pressure seawater system and the gas turbine seawater system. The former has a ring main that services the machinery spaces. It is fed by a pump capable of supplying all the equipment cooled by the system with 200m³/h of seawater

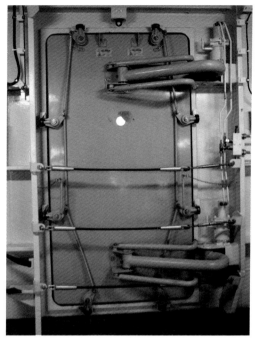

at 340kPa. A second, identical pump is always on automatic standby should the first fail. At action stations the ring main can be divided into forward and aft sections each supplied by its own pump. The system provides cooling water to the high-pressure air compressors, all the components of the main shaft lines, the stabilisers and the GTA's systems. The gas turbine seawater system cools the gas turbine's intercoolers and lubricating oil. The two low-pressure systems have identical pumps. Consequently, in an emergency, the low-pressure seawater system can also supply the gas turbine with cooling water.

Chilled water (CW) system

Virtually all the electricity supplied to ship's equipment by the 440V AC electrical distribution system is turned into heat; only a small fraction of the energy is emitted as radar or communications signals. This heat is removed by chilled water, either by means of heat exchangers in electronic cabinets or by cooling the compartment air surrounding the equipment.

There are four CW plants, two in each of the forward and aft machinery rooms. These reduce the temperature of demineralised water to 6.5°C by extracting heat. The heat is transferred to seawater and hence to the surrounding sea. The CW is circulated around a main on 2-Deck

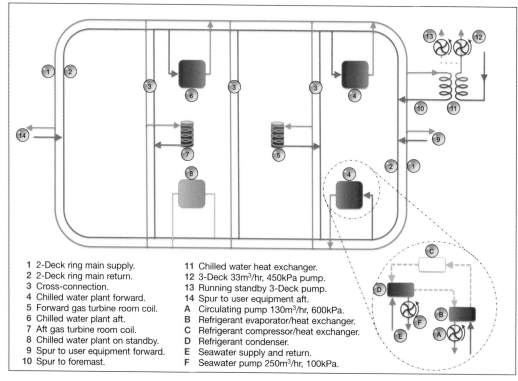

1 2-Deck ring main supply.
2 2-Deck ring main return.
3 Cross-connection.
4 Chilled water plant forward.
5 Forward gas turbine room coil.
6 Chilled water plant aft.
7 Aft gas turbine room coil.
8 Chilled water plant on standby.
9 Spur to user equipment forward.
10 Spur to foremast.
11 Chilled water heat exchanger.
12 3-Deck 33m³/hr, 450kPa pump.
13 Running standby 3-Deck pump.
14 Spur to user equipment aft.
A Circulating pump 130m³/hr, 600kPa.
B Refrigerant evaporator/heat exchanger.
C Refrigerant compressor/heat exchanger.
D Refrigerant condenser.
E Seawater supply and return.
F Seawater pump 250m³/hr, 100kPa.

comprising two rings of pipework – one to supply CW and one to return it to the plant. Coolant is drawn from the ring main's supply pipework and fed to equipment's heat exchangers. Having cooled the equipment, the warmer water (at approximately 13.5°C) flows back through the return pipework. Depending on the heat generated within the ship, the number of operational CW plants is varied. There are spurs forward and aft of the main to supply coolant to equipment sited at the forecastle and aft of the ship. For emergency use there are a number of automatic and manual valves to isolate sections of the system and three cross-connections to provide flexibility. There is additional cooling for the gas turbine rooms for times when the ship is at action stations and closed down so that downtake air cannot be used to cool the compartment.

To cool the Sampson MFR and RESM equipment in compartments on the higher decks of the foremast there are two boost pumps on 3-Deck to circulate CW through those compartments. To guard against failure, one is operational while a second is on standby. Because of the additional pressure needed to supply coolant to the higher decks this circuit is isolated from the ring main by a CW to CW heat exchanger.

Each CW plant has an open drive, rotary-screw compressor. The compressor's flange-mounted motor has an hydraulically actuated capacity control that smoothly varies between 10% and 100%. The plant has a vertical spindle, constant speed, electrically driven pump to circulate the CW. Cooling seawater is circulated through the plant by a similar pump.

Chilled water plant characteristics	
Dimensions (L x W x H)	4.5m x 2.3m x 2.35m
Weight	13,000kg
Cooling capacity	1,100kW
Temperature (output/return)	6.5°C/13.5°C
Output pressure	400 to 600kPa
Output volume	Up to 130m³/h

Heating, ventilation and air conditioning (HVAC) system

The HVAC system provides the ship's complement with a plentiful supply of safe air at a comfortable temperature and humidity. It is divided into four autonomous zones. To ventilate the ship, fresh (but often humid) air is drawn in through intakes high on the superstructure (in order to prevent sea spray and pre-wetting mist from being ingested). The air from each of the intakes is ducted to an air filtration unit that passes it through a pre-particulate filter and then, in normal operation, through a particulate filter. If there is a possibility of a CBRN attack then an alternative filter is used to remove harmful agents. Much of the air within the ship is recirculated, but some air naturally leaks from the ship through doorways open to the atmosphere. The air from the air filtration unit replaces this air lost from the ship and is referred to as 'make-up air'. The filtered fresh air passes to one of 19 air conditioning units spread throughout the ship, several being allocated to each zone. In each air conditioning unit the air is first mixed with recirculated air and their combined airflow again filtered. The air is then cooled in a chiller, where water vapour within the air condenses (thereby reducing the air's humidity), before the air is heated to a comfortable temperature. A fan unit forces the air through deckhead ducting, delivering it to compartments to ventilate the ship. Stale air is extracted under the suction produced by the recirculating fans. Air ventilating sanitary spaces does not re-enter the ship without being disinfected by an ultraviolet system in the

LEFT A louvred air filter unit intake (centre). *(Airfix)*

extraction ducting. Extracted air is returned to the air conditioning unit for recirculation.

To help cool the ship there are 14 fan coil units in those operational compartments that are likely to overheat. Cooled by the CW

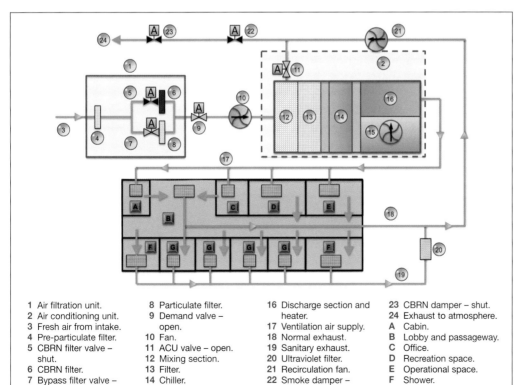

1 Air filtration unit.	**8** Particulate filter.	**16** Discharge section and heater.	**23** CBRN damper – shut.
2 Air conditioning unit.	**9** Demand valve – open.	**17** Ventilation air supply.	**24** Exhaust to atmosphere.
3 Fresh air from intake.	**10** Fan.	**18** Normal exhaust.	**A** Cabin.
4 Pre-particulate filter.	**11** ACU valve – open.	**19** Sanitary exhaust.	**B** Lobby and passageway.
5 CBRN filter valve – shut.	**12** Mixing section.	**20** Ultraviolet filter.	**C** Office.
6 CBRN filter.	**13** Filter.	**21** Recirculation fan.	**D** Recreation space.
7 Bypass filter valve – open.	**14** Chiller.	**22** Smoke damper – shut.	**E** Operational space.
	15 Fan section.		**F** Shower.
			G Heads.

LEFT Simplified schematic of heating, ventilation and air conditioning system configured for seagoing operations.

(Author)

Fresh-water (FW) systems

Each member of the ship's company requires about 260 litres of fresh water daily for drinking, cooking, laundry, washing and sanitation purposes. To provide the quantities of FW required for such domestic uses, the ship produces it from seawater. Three FW plants remove both suspended and dissolved solids from the seawater. Suspended solids are made up of a wide range of materials – mineral sediments, organic matter and microorganisms. Particles that would settle out of still water are kept in suspension in seawater because of its constant motion. Dissolved solids, mainly inorganic salts and some organic compounds, are very much smaller than suspended solids, with sizes on the molecular level. The seawater also contains biological species, including parasites, bacteria and viruses, that must be removed to ensure the water is safe to drink (potable).

The production of FW is achieved using sequential processes; a pre-treatment stage to remove solids and two reverse osmosis stages to remove dissolved salts. The equipment for both processes and their accompanying equipment, such as pumps and a control panel, are supplied as a single unit.

The pre-treatment process removes particles that would damage the later reverse osmosis stage. It is a crossflow micro-filter designed to cope with challenging and variable raw seawater conditions. Raw seawater is pumped through a strainer (to remove any large pieces of debris) and a micro-filter membrane. The micro-filter

system, these units cut in automatically to reduce the temperature of the compartment air to a predetermined level.

In the event of a fire, air is not supplied to the affected area. Once the fire is extinguished air is not recirculated but, to clear the smoke, is vented through the smoke damper to the atmosphere.

Machinery spaces are normally ventilated by air that is not conditioned. It is drawn in by fans through jalousie separators in the superstructure. The exhaust air is removed by other fans and returned to the atmosphere through other vents in the superstructure. All the inlet and exhaust fan housings and ducting are fitted with cooling coils, fire dampers and CBRN dampers. When the dampers are closed, heat is removed by fan coil units in the machinery spaces.

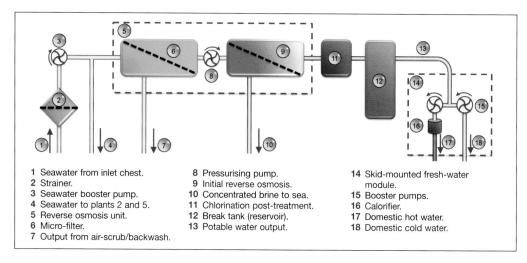

RIGHT Elements of the fresh-water system. *(Author from Pall Corp information)*

1 Seawater from inlet chest.
2 Strainer.
3 Seawater booster pump.
4 Seawater to plants 2 and 5.
5 Reverse osmosis unit.
6 Micro-filter.
7 Output from air-scrub/backwash.

8 Pressurising pump.
9 Initial reverse osmosis.
10 Concentrated brine to sea.
11 Chlorination post-treatment.
12 Break tank (reservoir).
13 Potable water output.

14 Skid-mounted fresh-water module.
15 Booster pumps.
16 Calorifier.
17 Domestic hot water.
18 Domestic cold water.

pore structure cannot be penetrated by particles and colloids larger than 100nm. As with most crossflow filters, the seawater is passed through tubes of a semi-permeable membrane. Filtrate is collected on the outside of the tubes.

Despite passing the raw seawater continuously over the membrane, the filtration membrane retains solids, so an increase in trans-membrane pressure is required to maintain the flow. To reduce the operating pressure and restore the effectiveness of the membrane, it is regularly purged using simultaneous air-scrub/reverse filtration. During this process, previously filtered water is passed through the tubes to wash particles from the membrane. Meanwhile, small bubbles of air are passed over the outside of the fibres to scour any particles from the membrane. For high-volume water treatment this may be done several times a day. Such purging is supplemented by other 'clean in place' techniques such as daily treatment with chlorine cleaner and a monthly clean with both chlorine and sodium hydroxide.

The membrane is sufficiently fine to remove suspended solids and to form a micro-biological barrier to prevent microorganisms, pathogens and most viruses from passing to the next stage. Such pre-treatment reduces biological fouling of the reverse osmosis membranes and delays scale formation, thereby maintaining the effectiveness and extending the life of downstream equipment.

To produce FW, dissolved solids are removed from the pre-treated water by passing it, under pressure, over a reverse osmosis membrane. This membrane is even finer than the micro-filter and is contained in a cylindrical module. The feed-water passes over several disc-shaped sections of membrane in turn. Pure water permeates the membrane leaving salt-rich brine behind. As FW is extracted the feed-water thus becomes increasingly saline and, having passed through the reverse osmosis module, this concentrate is discarded.

The cylindrical modules use short feed-flow paths, open channels and high packing densities to minimise concentration, polarisation and physical flow impediments. This reduces scaling and fouling, ensuring that efficiency is maintained. Unlike the earlier sealed, spirally wound and hollow-fibre membrane systems, the disc system can be dismantled.

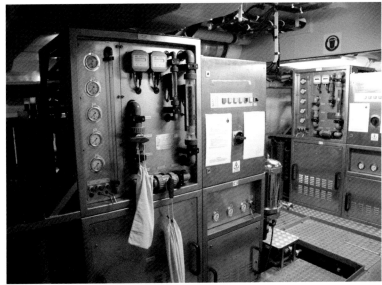

ABOVE Two reverse osmosis plants with integrated pre-treatment. *(Crown Copyright, 2012 HMS Defender)*

RIGHT Photo of disc tube reverse osmosis cylindrical module. *(Pall Corp)*

BELOW Principle of (a) reverse osmosis micro-filter and (b) simultaneous air-scrub/reverse filtration. *(Author from Pall Corp information)*

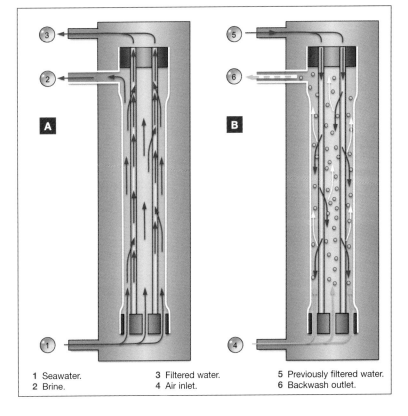

| 1 Seawater. | 3 Filtered water. | 5 Previously filtered water. |
| 2 Brine. | 4 Air inlet. | 6 Backwash outlet. |

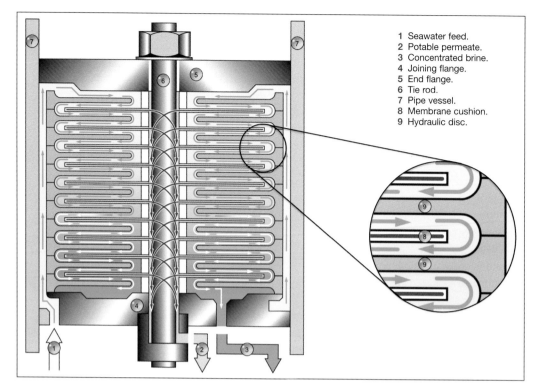

1 Seawater feed.
2 Potable permeate.
3 Concentrated brine.
4 Joining flange.
5 End flange.
6 Tie rod.
7 Pipe vessel.
8 Membrane cushion.
9 Hydraulic disc.

This allows inspection of the membrane and the replacement of individual sheets of membrane rather than a whole unit.

Domestic FW is distributed from two identical skid packages, one located forward and one aft, which supply cold and hot water to their respective ring mains on 2-Deck. The packages are interconnected by a bypass system that enables one unit to supply all the domestic water needs if necessary. Each skid comprises a 440-litre, 240kW calorifier, cold and hot water pumps, expansion vessels, a control panel and all associated control valves.

While the reverse osmosis process produces water that is safe to drink, a second reverse osmosis stage is used to produce even purer technical water. This is used for diesel generator and CW header tanks and for washing of the gas turbines and helicopters.

Waste-water treatment

Both sewage (black water) and water that has been used for washing (grey water) are treated on board so that the ship's output meets the exacting environmental standards for discharge to the ocean. Sewage is collected by a vacuum-assisted collection and transfer system and delivered to the sewage treatment plants. Grey water is piped by gravity feed to the same plants that are capable of treating all waste water produced when the maximum number of personnel are aboard. The treatment plant uses membrane bioreactor technology to purify both types of waste water using a combination of biological degradation and membrane separation. The process mixes the waste with a biomass of aerobic bacteria that digest the waste in the presence of air. Clean water is discharged to the ocean, odourless air and water vapour are released to the atmosphere. This technique achieves high standards without the use of chemicals.

Reverse osmosis plant key characteristics	
System process components dimensions (L x W x H)	1.49m x 1.20m x 1.95m
System process components weight	1,260kg
Reverse osmosis modules dimensions (L x W x H)	1.74m x 1.14m x 1.50m
Reverse osmosis modules weight	1,400kg
Pre-treatment micro-filtration membrane modules	2
Reverse osmosis stainless steel cylinders	10
Total reverse osmosis membrane area	76.5m^2
Reverse osmosis pressure	12MPa
Nominal fresh-water production per plant	35m^3/day
Fresh-water storage (fore and aft tanks)	140 tonnes

The operation of the membrane bioreactor waste-water treatment plant is shown diagrammatically. The liquid mixture of sewage and grey water waste is delivered to the first-stage bioreactor, where it is aerated to begin the purification process. Liquid from this reactor is pumped to an interstage filter. Solids from the filter (screenings) are returned for further processing, whereas the filtered liquid is pumped to a larger second-stage reactor for further purification as aerated biomass. Biomass liquid is withdrawn and pumped to a series of GRP filtration modules containing large numbers of ultrafiltration membrane tubes. As the biomass passes under pressure through the tubes, purified water permeates the membrane and is collected from the module. It is important that the velocity of the liquid travelling through the tubes is sufficient to reduce the risk of blockage. This concentrated biomass is returned to the second-stage reactor for further processing. The purified water collected is stored for eventual discharge. The design anticipated more rigorous regulation, so purification levels meet the latest Marine Environment Protection Committee standard that applies to plants installed after 2009.

The bilge and sullage system collects, stores and treats waste water that accumulates in the lower spaces of the hull as well as water from the fuel stripping systems. Such water is contaminated with oil, grease and detergents but, after treatment, the water meets International Maritime Organisation standards and can be discharged overboard. There are also temporary emergency bilge pumps for direct discharge of bilge water in the case of severe flooding.

Waste water treatment plant key characteristics	
Dimensions (L x W x H)	4.76m x 3.91m x 1.85m
Weight (dry)	9,350kg
Weight (wet)	20,200kg
Raw sewage input	2.35m³/day
Grey sewage input	51.7m³/day
Biochemical oxygen demand input	20kg/day
Number of membrane modules per plant	6
Total bioreactor tank volume	10.5m³

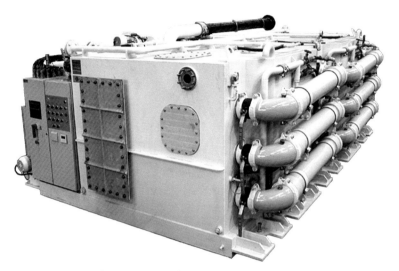

ABOVE Membrane bioreactor waste water treatment plant. **BELOW** A membrane bioreactor tube. *(Wärtsilä Hamworthy)*

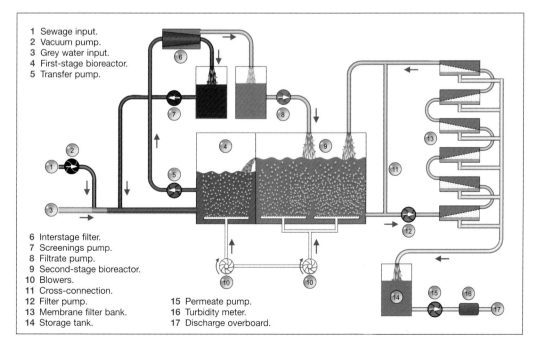

1 Sewage input.
2 Vacuum pump.
3 Grey water input.
4 First-stage bioreactor.
5 Transfer pump.

6 Interstage filter.
7 Screenings pump.
8 Filtrate pump.
9 Second-stage bioreactor.
10 Blowers.
11 Cross-connection.
12 Filter pump.
13 Membrane filter bank.
14 Storage tank.

15 Permeate pump.
16 Turbidity meter.
17 Discharge overboard.

LEFT Schematic of membrane bioreactor waste water treatment plant. *(Author from Wärtsilä Hamworthy information)*

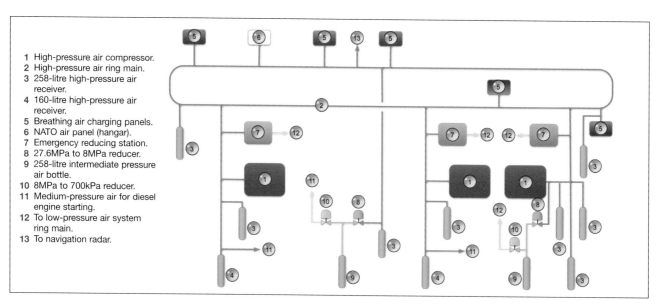

1 High-pressure air compressor.
2 High-pressure air ring main.
3 258-litre high-pressure air receiver.
4 160-litre high-pressure air receiver.
5 Breathing air charging panels.
6 NATO air panel (hangar).
7 Emergency reducing station.
8 27.6MPa to 8MPa reducer.
9 258-litre intermediate pressure air bottle.
10 8MPa to 700kPa reducer.
11 Medium-pressure air for diesel engine starting.
12 To low-pressure air system ring main.
13 To navigation radar.

ABOVE Schematic of high-pressure air system (air supply and shore supply omitted for simplification).
(Author)

High-pressure air system

Compressed air has a wide range of applications on modern surface warships. Low-pressure air (up to 1MPa) is used for general service and to dry wave-guides of conventional radars (which prevents arcing). The advantage of compressed air is that it can be stored in cylinders to provide an instant, independent source of power. Medium-pressure air (up to 4MPa) is used for diesel engine starting, whereas high-pressure air (up to 35MPa), is employed for gas turbine starting. High-pressure air also provides power for torpedo launching, is used in support of the helicopter and to charge breathing sets employed by divers and firefighters.

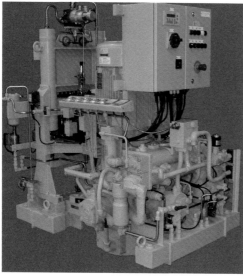

RIGHT WP5500 water-cooled high-pressure air compressor.
(JP Sauer)

Traditionally there have been several small, dedicated compressors covering each of the three pressure ranges. However, the Type 45 destroyers have a centralised system delivering all the ship's compressed air from three high-pressure air compressors. This type of compressor, once unreliable and expensive, is now dependable and offers savings in overall weight and space, initial cost, logistical support and maintenance. To reduce the vulnerability of the system, these three compressors and their associated storage cylinders are sited at three different locations in the ship. A ring main running through the ship connects the compressors and supplies all equipment requiring high-pressure compressed air, if necessary after the pressure has been adjusted. Low-pressure air is derived from the high-pressure system through reducing stations and is supplied to appropriate equipment by means of a low-pressure ring main.

High-pressure compressor characteristics	
Dimensions (L x W x H)	970mm x 810mm x 1,325mm
Weight	930kg
Stages	4 (0.6, 2, 9.5, 27.6MPa)
Cylinders	4 radial
Power input	22kW
Output pressure	27.6MPa
Output volume	53m³/h
Speed	1,170rpm at 60Hz

The four-stage high-pressure air compressor is based on a commercial design and cooled by seawater. It has a unique feature – a vertical crankshaft with four cylinders radially arranged around it to reduce vibration and structure-borne noise. The compressor's oil, water and air spaces are hermetically separated and dry-lined. A maintenance-free interstage membrane dehydrator between the third and fourth stages uses semi-permeable membranes to eliminate water vapour from the compressed air without resort to maintenance-intensive desiccant dryers. These techniques allow the compressor to deliver oil-free dry air.

Firefighting systems

The fire, smoke and flood detection system incorporates a series of digital detectors that provide early warning of the outbreak of flood, fire, or both. The destroyers are equipped with several systems tailored to extinguish the type of conflagration that may occur in different compartments:

■ Main machinery rooms and switchboard rooms have a fixed firefighting system that can extinguish fires in adjacent spaces by drenching them with carbon dioxide (CO_2) gas under pressure. Two compartments, forward and aft, each store 45 CO_2 cylinders of which 8 cylinders supply the adjoining gas turbine enclosure while 4 are connected to the nearby diesel generator enclosure. Before a compartment is drenched, all ventilation is 'crash stopped' and an alarm sounds. The alarm ensures that personnel within the compartment don breathing apparatus because the concentration of CO_2 required to extinguish a fire is lethal. When the fire is extinguished CO_2 is cleared from the compartment or enclosure by the ventilation fans.

■ The primary fire protection system for compartments that store fuel (the hangar, the aviation category fuel pump room and the emergency generator room) is a fixed firefighting system that generates aqueous firefighting foam. This also operates as a secondary fire suppression system for the eight main machinery rooms. The system has two identical and separate halves that can, in an emergency, be cross-connected. The 1% non-aspirating foam is produced at the rate of 10 litres/min/m³ by mixing concentrate with seawater. When the foam is depleted the system can use seawater spray supplied by the HPSW system.

■ In case of a helicopter crash on the flight deck, two remotely operated monitors can envelop the flight deck in aqueous firefighting foam within two minutes and continue to spray foam for a further ten minutes. When the foam is depleted they change to spraying seawater.

■ Most magazines are protected by the rapid reaction spray system. Each magazine has a fully automatic fire detection system with at least three heat sensors. Should the magazine temperature exceed 60°C the system is activated. Small magazines that require only one or two nozzles have a fully charged quartzoid bulb spray system. The bulbs fracture at 68°C, allowing HPSW to spray the magazine.

■ Compartments not protected by the fixed systems above, but which nevertheless contain some flammable material (such as accommodation areas), are fitted with a manually activated HPSW spray. Modular cabin units have void spaces between them and the ship's steel bulkheads. These voids (and the space beneath the accommodation modules) are fitted with a dry (normally empty) spray pipe with open nozzles that can be activated in the case of a fire to boundary-cool the outside of the modules.

ABOVE Port firefighting foam monitor on aft superstructure. *(Crown Copyright, 2012 HMS Defender)*

BELOW Testing of flight-deck firefighting foam monitor during outfitting. *(Steve Wagstaff)*

Chapter Three

Anatomy of the combat system

Destroyers provide vital defence for groups of ships against air attack. Several sophisticated sensors enable them to be vigilant to potential threats; missiles and a variety of guns allow them to engage even the most formidable air threats. Powerful computers enable engagements to be efficiently controlled by a small highly-trained team.

OPPOSITE HMS *Defender*'s Sea Viper system launches an Aster-15 missile for the first time on 15 May 2014 against a Mirach drone. The Sampson multi-function radar (the large spherical object on top of the mast structure) both tracks the target and controls the missile engagement. *(MBDA UK)*

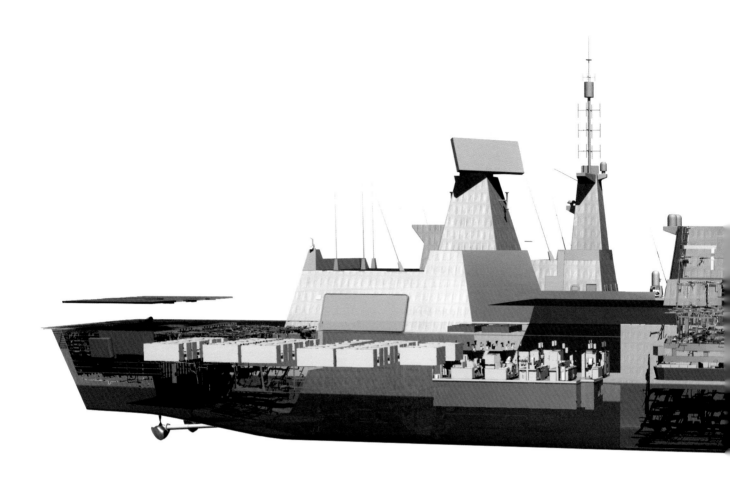

Combat system weapons and sensors.

(Author)

1 Sea Viper anti-air warfare system comprising:
   a Sylver A-50 launcher.
   b Aster-30 missiles.
   c Aster-15 missiles.
   d Sea Viper local command and control.
   e Sampson multifunction radar Type 1045.
2 Mk8 Mod 1 medium-calibre gun.
3 Outfit DLH launchers (port and starboard).

4 Combat management system.
5 Outfit DLF(3) Seagnat launchers.
6 Small-calibre gun (port and starboard).
7 20mm Block 1B Phalanx gun (port and starboard).
8 Miniguns (port and starboard).
9 General-purpose machine guns (port and starboard).

A Sampson multifunction radar Type 1045.

B Outfit UAT radar electronic surveillance measures.
C I-band navigation radar Type 1047.
D E/F-band surface search radar Type 1048.
E Electro-optic sensor system.
F Long-range radar Type 1046.
G IFF interrogator radar Type 1018.
H IFF transponder radar Type 1019 (port and starboard).
I Medium frequency sonar.
J Lynx helicopter.

ABOVE Cutaway of Type 45 destroyer. *(Alex Pang)*

The Operations Complex

The warship's combat system comprises sensors to detect and analyse potential threats, weapons to destroy hostile targets and decoys to confuse the enemy's incoming missiles. The command team controls the combat system principally from the Operations Complex.

The Operations Complex comprises a suite of compartments on 02-Deck containing all the equipment and facilities necessary to plan and execute offensive and defensive operations:

■ *The Operations Room* – the destroyer's nerve centre, from which the command team conducts real-time battle management and from which internal and external communications are managed.
■ *The CMS Equipment Office* (or Computer Room), which houses computers and

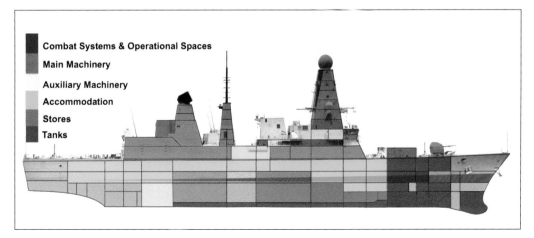

Combat Systems & Operational Spaces
Main Machinery
Auxiliary Machinery
Accommodation
Stores
Tanks

LEFT Functional space allocation highlighting the combat system and operational spaces. *(Author from BAE Systems information)*

ABOVE HMS
Diamond's command
team in the Operations
Room during work-up.
*(Crown Copyright, 2011
PO(Phot) Paul Punter)*

BELOW Sir Patrick
Stewart on a visit
to the *Star Trek*-like
Operations Room on
HMS *Daring*. *(Crown
Copyright, 2010 Kristen
Whalen Somody)*

communications equipment that supports the CMS.

■ *Two communications equipment rooms* containing the communications equipment to support internal and external communications.

■ *The Joint Planning Room*, a versatile operations space for use by embarked forces' officers for planning and briefing of operations.

■ *The Embarked Forces Planning Room.*

Space has also been allocated for potential future equipment such as communications electronic support measures.

The Operations Room contains 22 combat management system (CMS-1) multifunction consoles to display all the information necessary to handle tactical data, analyse the operational situation and control the weapons. They also

enable the command team to appreciate and manage the wider task force context. CMS-1 design represents a quantum leap in comparison to previous operations rooms and has been compared to the futuristic command decks of vessels from the fictional *Star Trek* films.

The responsibilities of individuals within the command team are similar to those of personnel on earlier ships, but these tasks have become more complex. However, technology has made greater flexibility of action possible and significant increases in computer-based automation now assist the operators in performing their tasks. For example, the main radars can detect and provide information about several hundred potential threats within a range of about 400km. CMS-1 automates much of the task of merging data, classifying threats and compiling the tactical picture – the first stage of threat evaluation.

The Operations Room consoles are arranged around the Commanding Officer's console, from which the Captain can take command of the ship. The Principal Warfare Officer on his right takes charge of the details of fighting the ship. Some of the command team concentrate on condensing the operational information into 'situational pictures' depicting the above-water, surface and below-water circumstances, while other operators control the missiles, guns, decoys and electronic warfare equipment from their consoles. All of the multifunction consoles are extremely flexible. Different systems can be controlled concurrently on a single console, allowing, for instance, one operator to control both the SCGs and the MCG. If a console fails or is damaged, some functions may be sacrificed in order to maintain whichever roles are vital during the emergency.

The multifunction consoles make an immediate visible impact. Although the consoles can all be configured to perform a range of functions appropriate to their operator, they all have the same basic hardware configuration. Each has three high-resolution, flat-panel liquid crystal displays. The main, central 23in display is 1,600 x 1,200px and is flanked by two 18in 1,280 x 1,240px displays, the left display showing status data and the right display showing operational data. A keyboard, 14in touchpad, two communications Voice User

Units (VUUs) and tracker-ball (equivalent to a computer mouse) are provided for operator input. All are designed to be operated when wearing anti-flash gear donned at action stations. Two electronics pedestals support the desk and incorporate powerful computers and software needed to control the complex graphical displays. The right-hand pedestal houses computer processor units that provide combat system, secondary data display and video data display functionality. The left-hand pedestal contains processors running one of five possible additional sets of applications appropriate to the operators who use the console. The consoles' computers use the Windows 2000 security-enhanced operating system. The CMS architecture includes similar computers located in the equipment room nearby and running on the same operating system. Middleware separates the underlying display operating systems from the bespoke combat system applications.

The high degree of automation afforded by the communications equipment means there is no longer a need for a separate Main Communications Office, a feature of previous RN warships, as all communications traffic can be supervised and managed from only three consoles located in the Operations Room.

In addition to the command system, CMS-1 comprises the command support system and the secondary data display. The former displays strategic intelligence, in both textual and graphical form, and provides facilities to assist interpretation. It also enables the ship to participate in strategic command and control information systems and displays the wide area picture. It is a self-contained system using the UNIX operating system, with terminals in the Operations Room and Joint Planning Room.

The secondary data display handles operational and navigational data relating to the ship and its environment, simultaneously displaying a common set of such data to a number of users. It replaces the state-boards of earlier ships.

The DTS provides the high-speed, digital, inter-communication data highway between CMS-1 and the combat system equipment. It is the means by which CMS-1 exchanges tactical data and management information with, and

LEFT Assistant Above-Water Warfare Officer wearing anti-flash gear and fighting the ship from a CMS-1 multifunction console. *(Crown Copyright, 2011 PO(Phot) Paul Punter)*

controls, the ship's sensors and weapons. This DTS comprises a triple-redundant fibre-optic, high-speed Ethernet local area network capable of interfacing with member sub-systems. Couplers provide the direct interface between the DTS and combat system equipment that uses standard transmission control protocol and Internet protocol. Each of the three redundant networks sends real-time traffic independently. The receiving couplers discard replicated data.

Legacy equipment (equipment pre-dating the Type 45 destroyers) that has obsolescent

BELOW CMS-1 multifunction console. *(Author/BAE Systems photo)*

1 Main tactical display.
2 Secondary tactical display.
3 Auxiliary tactical display.
4 Trackerball.
5 Softkey panel.
6 Keyboard.
7 Right-hand pedestal.
8 Left-hand pedestal.

interfaces cannot access the DTS directly. Data for such equipment is carried to and from the DTS by a second triple-redundant system, the 'combat system highway' used on earlier warships. The large amount of video data generated by the ship's navigation and search radars (including IFF – identification friend or foe – information) is carried on a separate data network, the video distribution system.

Key to coordinating all the data handled within the ship (and that shared through external data-links) is ensuring that all data is accurately referred to a precise time. The warship's 'clock' for these purposes is the precise time and frequency equipment. This uses Coordinated Universal Time obtained from the NAVSTAR GPS satellite. Even if the NAVSTAR signal is absent for 45 days, Outfit FSF will maintain precise time to an accuracy of better than 250μsec. The high reliability of the system is achieved by dual redundancy of the internal rubidium frequency source. A phase-lock–loop control system ensures the high stability of each rubidium oscillator circuit.

RIGHT Sampson multifunction radar Type 1045. *(Steve Wagstaff)*

Sampson multifunction radar Type 1045 characteristics	
Frequency	E/F-band (2 to 4GHz)
Range	400km
Antenna	Rotating two planar active phased arrays in spheroid housing
Array dimensions	2.6m x 2.6m
Antenna diameter	5m maximum
Antenna centre	37.5m from waterline (radar horizon of about 25km)
Rotation rate	30rpm
Weight	Two antenna assemblies, each 4,800kg; mast equipment 2,500kg

Sea Viper (Guided Weapon System 45)

The Type 45 destroyer's main armament is Sea Viper, an AAW surface-to-air missile system, developed under a tri-national programme by France, Italy and the UK. With multiple channels of fire, Sea Viper can defend the vessels of a task force against a range of hostile air threats such as highly manoeuvrable incoming aircraft and missiles, including high-speed sea-skimming missiles. It thus provides an air defence umbrella for the destroyer and its consorts over a large area.

Sea Viper comprises several sensors and weapons:

- A Sampson multifunction radar Type 1045.
- Six Sylver A50 launchers, each with eight missile cells.
- Command and control software and dedicated terminals.
- A mixture of Aster-15 and Aster-30 missiles.

The LRR Type 1046 is also associated with Sea Viper, although it is not part of the system.

Sampson multifunction radar (MFR) Type 1045

The distinctive rotating Sampson MFR, mounted on top of the foremast high above the waterline, is an active, electronically scanned, phased-array radar operating in the E/F-band. It performs air and surface raster-like volume searches using innovative digital adaptive beam-forming techniques. These searches provide an accurate, high-definition, 3D plot and surveillance-track data to the Sea Viper system and to the ship's CMS. In addition to simultaneously tracking targets Sampson can control several Aster missiles in flight.

A major threat to any vessel comes from sea-skimming missiles fired by enemy submarines, ships and aircraft. These anti-ship missiles travel only a few metres above the sea's surface and can only be detected when they appear on the horizon. If a Type 45 destroyer is to protect ships in company with it its main radar must be as high as possible to maximise its radar horizon and so detect these threats at long range. Sampson MFR has to be light enough to be mounted on a high mast – a position that affords it full 360° coverage. Nevertheless, it has a large number of active elements needed to achieve the power, accuracy and performance necessary for long-range engagements. Sampson MFR meets these conflicting requirements by having two back-to-back rotating phased arrays. Each array has more than 2,000 gallium arsenide transmitter/receiver radiating elements, enabling it to rapidly form high-resolution narrow ('pencil') beams.

Software that shapes and directs its transmissions allows Sampson MFR to rapidly form the pencil beams allowing it to undertake multiple functions. The first function is the onerous task of surveillance – continuously scanning the skies and sea's surface with beams to detect targets ranging from high-flying aircraft at a distance of 400km to sea-skimming missiles. Unlike conventional radars, Sampson's beams can spend a greater time interrogating directions where intelligence suggests that threats may lie. Having detected and classified up to several hundred air, near surface and surface objects it can simultaneously track them. In addition, during an engagement Sampson MFR can communicate with several Aster missiles in flight, providing data on the positions and manoeuvres of their intended targets.

The large number of elements in the arrays means that Sampson MFR is robust, as it can adjust to the loss of some transmitter/receiver units. The antenna beam pattern exhibits very low side-lobes and a wide bandwidth that together make the radar inherently resistant to jamming. Furthermore, the ability to apply adaptive waveform control, frequency agility, side-lobe blanking and pulse compression allows it to be virtually immune to enemy countermeasures and deception tactics.

Power is provided to the rotating phased arrays through slip rings, and high-speed serial data signals are passed electro-optically. Its reliability is enhanced when compared to

RIGHT Cross-section of Sampson multifunction radar showing two array faces end-on and the airflows through the arrays. *(Author from BAE Systems information)*

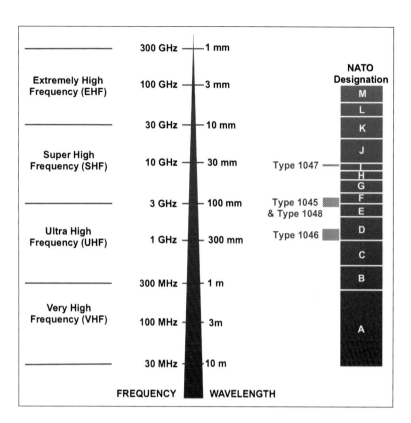

ABOVE Radar frequency designations. *(Author)*

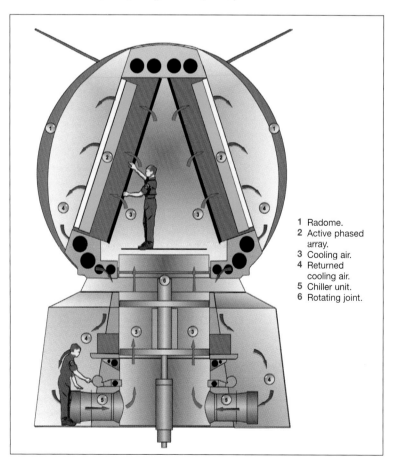

1 Radome.
2 Active phased array.
3 Cooling air.
4 Returned cooling air.
5 Chiller unit.
6 Rotating joint.

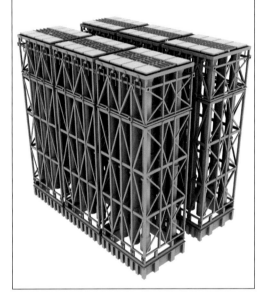

RIGHT Artist's impression of the assembly of six eight-cell Sylver modules. *(Alex Pang)*

conventional radars because Sampson MFR requires neither a rotating waveguide joint nor high-voltage components that are mechanical and electrical weak-points prone to failure. The antenna is cooled by air chilled in the masthead room immediately below the antenna.

Aster missiles and Sylver A50 launcher

Sea Viper's Aster missiles are stored on board in six Sylver A50 launcher modules each of which can accommodate eight missiles, allowing the destroyers to carry up to 48 missiles. The Sylver launchers are protected behind a raised coaming. Looking forward from the bridge these can be seen as two pairs of 12 missile cells running fore and aft.

A mixture of two types of anti-air missiles can be carried: Aster-15 missiles and Aster-30 missiles. Both types have two stages: a booster and a common terminal stage (the Dart). The booster of Aster-30 is taller, giving these missiles a longer range and higher speed than the Aster-15. Aster missiles are highly manoeuvrable, with an acceleration of 60g – 20 times more than a Formula One racing car. Within the launcher and for transport, each missile is contained within a nitrogen-filled canister that is rectangular in cross-section. As the Sylver launcher is tall enough for Aster-30 missiles, the shorter Aster-15 missiles are mounted on an adaptor. Within the canisters

RIGHT Sylver A-50 launcher (a) side and (b) end; (c) Aster-30 missile in canister; (d) Aster-30 wings folded; (e) Aster-30 wings deployed; (f) Aster-15 wings deployed; and (g) Aster-15 wings folded on adaptor. *(Author from MBDA information)*

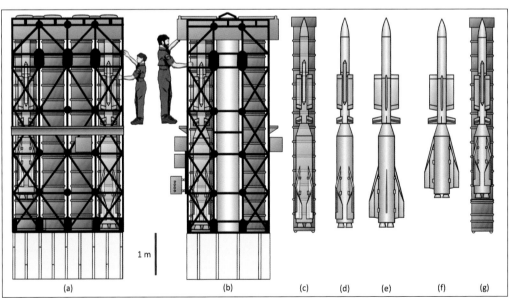

1 m

(a) (b) (c) (d) (e) (f) (g)

Sylver A50 vertical launch module characteristics	
Dimensions (L x W x H)	6m x 2.6m x 2.3m
including maintenance envelope	6m x 4.2m x 3.1m
Capacity	Eight Aster-15 or Aster-30 (or mixture)
Reloading time	< 90min for eight missiles

Aster-15 and Aster-30 characteristics		
	Aster-15	Aster-30
Dart length	2.7m	
Dart diameter	0.18m	
Dart wingspan	0.49m (main fins) 0.62m (rear fins)	
Dart weight	140kg	
Dart seeker	Active pulse-Doppler	
Dart warhead	10 to 15kg focused fragmentation	
Overall weight	310kg	450kg
Overall length	4.2m	4.9m
Booster diameter	0.36m	
Booster wingspan	0.42m (folded) 0.93m (unfolded in flight)	
Propulsion	solid propellant, two-stage	
Terminal speed	Mach 3 (1,000m/sec)	Mach 4.5 (1,500m/sec)
Manoeuvrability	> 60g	
Guidance	Data up-link and terminal phase active radar seeker	
Intercept altitude	13km	20km
Range	1.7km to over 30km	3km to over 100km
Canister weight	360kg	
Canister dimensions	5.0m x 0.55m x 0.55m	

the booster wings are folded, but are deployed once the missile is launched from the canister.

The Aster Dart is a long, slim cylinder with a sharply pointed nose. It has four slim, narrow chord wings in cruciform configuration and cropped-delta tail fins. Initial acceleration is provided by the booster, and when this has burnt its fuel the Dart uses its own sustainer motor to maintain flight towards its target.

The nose of the Dart contains a radar seeker with a high-power transmitter and wide-angle antenna. In the final approach this active radar searches for the designated target. Once it acquires the target the radar then locks on to and continuously tracks it to provide data on the target's relative position and motion for terminal guidance.

The Dart is controlled by a computer processing unit ('autopilot') that gathers data from the Dart's inertial guidance unit and from the sensors monitoring its functions. Mid-course it is provided with command up-link signals from

the warship and, as it approaches its target, inputs from its radar and proximity fuze. The autopilot processes the data and produces control signals for flight control, guidance and the sequencing of the missile's flight. When the proximity fuze senses the target it also initiates the firing of the warhead after a delay calculated to guarantee detonation at the optimum position. If necessary, on receipt of a correctly coded signal the unit commands the missile to self-destruct.

On the destroyer, Sea Viper has its own

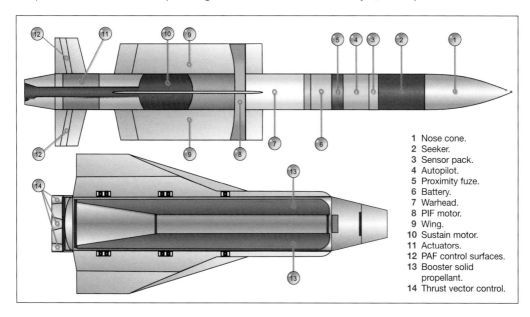

1 Nose cone.
2 Seeker.
3 Sensor pack.
4 Autopilot.
5 Proximity fuze.
6 Battery.
7 Warhead.
8 PIF motor.
9 Wing.
10 Sustain motor.
11 Actuators.
12 PAF control surfaces.
13 Booster solid propellant.
14 Thrust vector control.

LEFT Cutaway of common Aster missile Dart and booster for Aster-30. *(Author from MBDA information)*

unique command and control system that performs picture management, platform threat evaluation and weapon assignment, as well as engagement planning and control. It provides the primary interface with the CMS. The command and control software contains approximately 500,000 lines of code and runs on high-performance processing boards in a main processing unit. An identical unit acts as a 'hot' spare ready to take control on the command of a master switching unit. Sea Viper is controlled from consoles in the Operations Room, but the Sea Viper equipment room contains three identical multifunction consoles for reversionary use in an emergency.

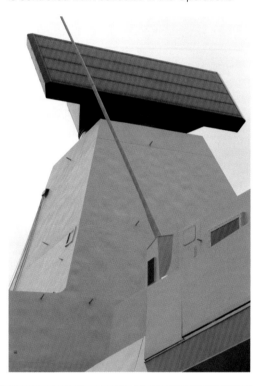

RIGHT Long-range radar Type 1046. *(Airfix)*

Long-range radar (LRR) Type 1046

The LRR is located on the forward part of the hangar superstructure. It is an updated version of radar fitted to the *Horizon* frigates, offering additional waveforms and improved counter-countermeasures (techniques to overcome the countermeasures employed by the enemy to confuse the destroyer's radar). The antenna is electronically stabilised, producing multiple beams up to a 70° elevation angle. The LRR is inhibited over a forward arc of about 12° in azimuth so that it does not illuminate (and consequently receive reflections from) the foremast.

The radar provides wide area search capability for Sea Viper and other ship systems, detecting objects within 400km of the ship. It is capable of fully automatic detection, track initiation and tracking of up to 1,000 air targets and providing 3D track and plot data to the CMS. Its platform threat evaluation and weapon assignment software can automatically send cues to the Sampson MFR so that it may start tracking potentially hostile targets identified by the LRR.

In cold conditions the LRR antenna is susceptible to the accumulation of ice and the freezing of the bearings and slip-rings. This is prevented by supplying water heated to 20°C to the antenna during such conditions.

The D-band IFF interrogator Type 1018 antenna mounted on the back of the radar emits civilian and military coded transmissions. Coded responses from friendly ships and aircraft assist the ship's CMS to distinguish long-range potential threats. The destroyers also have IFF transponders Type 1019 on the port and starboard main mast yardarms. These transponders emit the coded response when receiving coded signals by interrogators from friendly forces. To prevent damage to the ship's RESM sensors and IFF transponders, the LRR interrogator sends a pulse-blanking signal to these sensors whenever it is transmitting in their direction.

Long-range radar Type 1046 characteristics	
System role	Provides 3D plot and surveillance track data and IFF data
Frequency	D-band (1 to 2GHz) with vertical polarisation
Range	65km stealth missiles; 400km patrol aircraft
Antenna	Electronically stabilised with integrated D-band IFF mounted on back
Antenna elements	24 (16 transceivers, 8 receivers)
Beams	16 beams 2.2° horizontal and 0–70° vertical beam-width
Antenna dimensions	8.4m × 4.0m × 4.4m
Antenna height	26.5m from waterline
Weight	Overall 8,400kg; antenna assembly and mast equipment 7,800kg tonnes
Maximum targets	1,000 airborne; 100 seaborne tracked
Rotation rate	12rpm

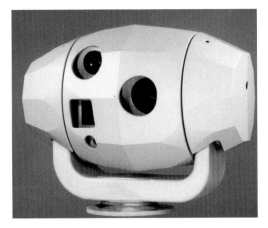

Electro-optical gunfire control system (EOGCS)

EOGCS provides command and control signals to both the MCG and the two SCGs. It undertakes surveillance, tracks potential targets and, for those identified as a threat, generates gunfire control solutions based on target motion analysis and prediction.

EOGCS's sensors are mounted on two electro-optical sensor platforms. Each platform has two forward-looking infrared sensors, detecting near infrared and mid-infrared wavelengths respectively, and a colour low-light optical TV camera. These sensors gather data day and night to warn of potentially hostile surface and air targets. They are capable of detecting high-performance combat aircraft and missiles at ranges of up to 18km. The two platforms are mounted port and starboard on the bridge roof so that their combined coverage allows them to simultaneously track and survey over the complete 360° arc. Their coverage overlaps over a forward 155° arc that includes the arc of fire of the MCG. As the sensors are passive they cannot determine target range, but each platform has an eye-safe laser rangefinder for this purpose. Data from the electro-optical sensors are distributed by the same system that distributes weather-deck CCTV signals.

EOGCS can be manually alerted to potential targets using a quick pointing device, a hand-held monocular viewing sight located on each bridge wing. It is used to identify a target's relative bearing and angle of sight as a cue to EOGCS.

The target information from EOGCS and from the navigation and search radars is used by the Surface Picture Supervisor to monitor and evaluate target tracks. Such data is used for kill assessments when the guns have engaged targets, as well as for navigation and

Electro-optical gunfire control system sensor platform characteristics	
System role	Target detection in optical and infrared
Forward-looking infrared	Resolution 640 x 480 pixels
3 to 5µm sensors	Platinum silicide focal-plane array
8 to 12µm sensors	Mercury cadmium telluride focal-plane array
Visible sensor	Colour TV, 10x optical zoom, 4x digital zoom
Range (fast aircraft)	18km
Laser rangefinder	Eye-safe
Stabilisation	Two axes

Medium-calibre gun (MCG) Mk8 Mod 1

The Type 45 destroyer's main gun is a 114mm (4.5in) Mk8 Mod 1 Naval MCG that entered service in 2001. The main purpose of the MCG is naval gunfire support in anti-surface warfare operations against land targets. In this role the gun is capable of firing the equivalent of a six-gun shore battery. It can also be used effectively against ships. MCG is capable of firing high-explosive rounds, chaff dispensing rounds, illumination rounds and also an improved munition, the base bleed high-explosive extended range round, with a range of 27.5km. The Mod 1 gun introduces improvements in gun technology such as electric drives and built-in test equipment. The most noticeable change is the multi-faceted gun-shield that is designed to reduce radar cross-section.

The MCG's turret is unoccupied during firing. A two-stroke chain hoist automatically delivers the appropriate ammunition from its ready-use storage position on a feed-ring sited immediately below the MCG in the gun-bay. The feed-ring is manually replenished with shells from the magazine in the gun-bay.

The Gun Controller, from his position in the Operations Room, selects the target and the

JACKSPEAK

The Mk8 Mod 1 gun has a gun-shield comprising a number of flat plates. This gun has been nicknamed 'Kryten', after the android in the television series *Red Dwarf* whose head has a similar appearance.

to control search and rescue operations. The EOGCS sensor data is processed by a gun control predictor. This passes information to the guns to allow them to rapidly adjust range and bearing settings, thereby increasing their accuracy. The predictor has much higher computing power than previous generations. This, combined with its detailed encyclopaedic range tables and interpolation algorithms, enables EOGCS to provide continuous accurate pointing predictions.

For the first time on a ship of the RN, the EOGCS allows both the MCG and the SCGs to be operated from a single remote console instead of by operators sitting on the gun mounts. This feature, developed especially for Type 45 destroyers, offers increased accuracy as well as improving the operator's safety.

LEFT Cutaway of the 114mm Mk8 Mod 1 medium-calibre gun. *(Alex Pang)*

BELOW The 114mm Mk8 Mod 1 medium-calibre gun firing during trials of HMS *Daring*; the yellow dashed line represents the area of danger from the gun slewing. *(BAE Systems)*

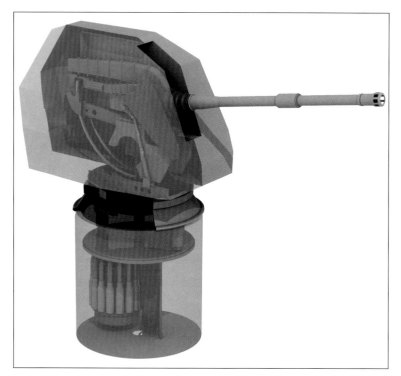

RIGHT Sailors on HMS *Dragon* loading shells on to the gun feed-ring of the medium-calibre gun in the gun-room immediately beneath the gun. *(Crown Copyright, 2012)*

type of shell to be loaded from the feed-ring. The EOGCS provides bearing and elevation of the gun barrel appropriate to the target, enabling the Gun Controller to fire the gun.

Small-calibre guns (SCGs)

SCGs are mounted on platforms port and starboard on 02-Deck, the two guns giving all-round coverage. Before the gun is used in action the stanchions carrying the safety nets around the platform are hinged down so the nets are level with the platform. The SCGs are 30mm 75-calibre Mark 46 Mod 1 single-barrel cannons. The primary mode is remote firing from the Operations Room, but if necessary a single operator can fire a SCG from the mount. With a range of 10km, their purpose is to engage

BELOW Starboard 30mm small-calibre gun on its 02-Deck platform. *(BAE Systems)*

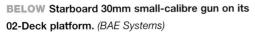

Medium-calibre gun characteristics		
System role	Naval gunfire support/large surface targets	
Single gun	114mm (6.2m barrel)	
Effective range	High-explosive extended range	27,500m
	High explosive	22,000m
Rate of fire	20 to 26r/min	
Ordnance weight (round/projectile)	High-explosive extended range	36.5kg/20.6kg
	High explosive	36.5kg/20.9kg
Bursting charge	High-explosive extended range	3kg RDX/TNT
Muzzle velocity	870m/sec	
Ammunition stowage	800 rounds	
Mount weight	27,200kg excluding ammunition	
Elevation	-10° to +55°	
Traverse	Approximately -155° to +155°	
Recoil	380mm	

Small-calibre gun characteristics		
System role	To engage surface and air close-in threats	
30mm single gun	Oerlikon 30mm/75 KCB cannon (2.25m barrel)	
Rifling	18 grooves 6° right-handed	
Operating mechanism	Gas-operated, air-cooled, link-belt fed	
Effective range	Anti-surface	10,000m
	Anti-air	2,750m
Rate of fire	Cyclic	650r/min
30mm ordnance (length 170mm)	High explosive	420g
	Armour-piercing discarding-sabot	300g
Muzzle velocity	High explosive	1,080m/sec
	Armour-piercing discarding-sabot	1,175m/sec
Ordnance	High-explosive incendiary with tracer	
Ammunition stowage	160 rounds	
Mount weight	1,200kg with ammunition	
Elevation	-20° to +65° at 55°/sec	
Traverse	360° at 55°/sec	

surface threats such as fast inshore attack craft, helicopters, unmanned aerial vehicles and other asymmetric threats. They are also used in policing operations against pirates and drug-runners. The DS30B Mk2 low radar and infrared signature mounts are electrically powered.

Phalanx close-in weapon system (CIWS) Mk15

Phalanx provides a gun-based, inner layer point defence capability against hostile anti-ship missiles and high-speed aircraft that have penetrated other fleet defences. Phalanx automatically detects, evaluates, tracks, engages, and performs kill assessment against such threats, thereby contributing to the destroyers' anti-air warfare capability.

Phalanx CIWS are mounted amidships on a 01-Deck port and starboard. They are on a protruding platform supported by a sponson from 1-Deck, enabling the two Phalanxes to give full 360° coverage. Phalanx is a self-contained system with its own radars and a six-barrelled Gatling gun, designed to destroy fast-moving nearby threats. The Gatling mechanism allows the very high rate of fire necessary against such targets. The search and track radar antennas are within the radome on top of the unit and all associated electronics for radar operations are enclosed within Phalanx.

Type 45 destroyers are fitted with Mk15 Phalanx Block 1B CIWS. This has the ability to counter asymmetric warfare threats through the addition of an integrated, stabilised electro-optical forward-looking infrared sensor that provides accurate angle-tracking information to the fire control computer. This upgrade, known as the Phalanx Surface Mode, enables Phalanx to detect and engage small high-speed surface craft, aircraft, helicopters, and unmanned aerial vehicles.

ABOVE Starboard 30mm small-calibre gun and Phalanx close-in weapons system with 03-Deck and 04-Deck forward down-take and up-take. *(Daniel Ferro)*

RIGHT Cutaway of Phalanx close-in weapons system. *(Alex Pang)*

Mk15 Phalanx 1B characteristics	
System role	Close-in self-defence gun (air and surface threats)
20mm gun	6-barrelled M61 Vulcan Gatling gun (barrel 2m)
Height	4.7m
Weight	6.2 tonnes
Effective range	Anti-air (missiles and aircraft) – 3,600m
Rate of fire (pneumatic feed)	Burst of up to 1,000 rounds at 50–75r/sec
Armour-penetrating ordnance	Tungsten 12.75mm discarding-sabot Overall 230g; projectile 100g
Muzzle velocity	1,100m/sec
Ammunition stowage	1,550 rounds per magazine
Mount weight	1,200kg with ammunition
Elevation	-25° to +85° at 115°/sec
Traverse	-150° to +150° at 116°/sec
Radar sensors	Upper search, lower tracking (12 to 18GHz region)
Electro-optical sensor	Side-mounted forward-looking infrared

Phalanx has also been integrated with the CMS to provide additional sensor and gunfire control information to other installed ship weapon systems. The installation of Phalanx 1B in HMS *Daring* represents the fifth and sixth fit of the 1B system to ships of the RN.

Small guns

The M134D Minigun is an electrically driven, air-cooled Gatling machine gun. It is a very high rate of fire 7.62mm weapon, giving it the high density of shot and the high accuracy needed to quickly suppress multiple targets. The guns are deployed, when needed, at strategic positions on the weather deck for use against close-in surface threats such as a terrorist attack. The position for the Minigun is armoured and further protection is given by the 30mm SCG platform above it on 02-Deck. The hose seen beneath the gun is the chute to dispose of spent casings when the gun is fired.

In addition to the Miniguns, Type 45 destroyers carry a number of gas-operated, belt-fed 7.62mm general-purpose machine guns (GPMGs) for use on the ship and its helicopter. The GPMGs are capable of firing 600 rounds per minute, with an effective range of 1.8km. These guns are used to defend the ship against attack in harbour and during transits of narrows or canals where the ship may come under small arms fire.

There are several mounting positions on the weather deck, including the forecastle and the seamanship openings of the enclosed quarterdeck. Each mount incorporates a cam that defines the arcs of fire allowable at that position. Temporary armour is also available for positions where the ship's structure does not offer protection.

Decoy launchers

Type 45 destroyers have two decoy launcher systems. The six-barrelled Seagnat launcher of Outfit DLH(2) on 02-deck deploy expendable rounds singly or as a group. Its software uses threat and countermeasures tables as well as command authorisation tables to determine which decoys to use and to tailor the response to a detected threat. The launchers have fixed

M134D Minigun characteristics	
System role	Manual close-support gun (air and surface threats)
Gun	6-barrelled Gatling gun (barrel 560mm)
Length	800mm
Weight	38.5kg
Effective range	<1,000m
Rate of fire	3,000r/min
Ordnance	7.62mm x 51mm
Muzzle velocity	853m/sec
Ammunition stowage	1,500, 3,000 or 4,400-round magazines

ABOVE A M134D Minigun with wrapped feed chute. *(Dillon Aero)*

LEFT Starboard 7.62mm M134D Minigun on 01-Deck beneath small-calibre gun platform. *(Daniel Ferro)*

LEFT General-purpose machine-gun position on forecastle behind removable armour. *(Daniel Ferro)*

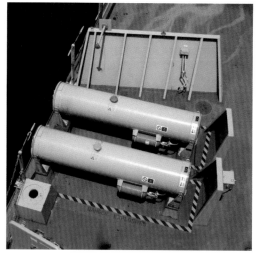

barrels angled at 45° elevation and aimed in azimuth at 30° and 105° from the ship's head. The four fixed launchers can deliver four types of decoy anti-radar chaff, infrared and active decoy rounds. These decoys, all of which weigh less than 30kg, are stored nearby in ready-use ammunition magazines and are manually loaded into the launcher.

The destroyers are also fitted with Outfit DLF(3) launchers port and starboard on the foredeck immediately forward of the superstructure. These dispense passive, naval off-board decoy system rounds. This is a rapid response countermeasure system deploying an expendable, inflatable, floating seduction decoy effective against radar-guided anti-ship missiles.

Radar electronic support measures (RESM) Outfit UAT(16)

The RESM system provides the destroyers with the ability to detect and identify potentially hostile air and surface units by means of their emitted radar signals – in some cases even before the fleet's radars can perceive them. The system has eight antennas so it can identify the threat direction, although, as a passive system, it provides no range information. Outfit UAT(16) features new signal processing and emitter identification technology. The pulse train of detected radars is analysed by a Minerva de-interleaver with an error rate significantly lower than earlier versions. Minerva uses the vast computing power of a neural net of 1,000

parallel processors to test a large number of ways of associating the pulses before selecting the most appropriate one. This technique gives a high detection rate and great fidelity. By comparing these characteristics to those in its database, the system can distinguish the radar type, so determining if it is likely to be on a hostile or friendly asset. RESM complements the IFF system's ability to identify friendly units.

Starting with HMS *Daring* in 2012, new digital antennas (Outfit UAT Mod 2) were fitted to the class.

Fully integrated communications system (FICS) Type FICS45

The communications system of a major warship such as HMS *Daring* is both vital and complex. The ship not only needs to exchange messages with the military command structure from anywhere within the world, but also to communicate with local civil authorities and with forces in its area of operations. These include ships in company, helicopters, aircraft, land forces and special forces.

Within the ship there are many operational positions that need to communicate with each other and with the outside world. FICS 45 provides a high integrity communication system with flexible connectivity between external and internal systems. It makes maximum use of automation and provides for interoperability with both military and civil authorities. The facilities for voice and data communications are provided over external terrestrial radio or satellite paths. It also supports a full range of internal voice communications, video and telephone services. A Communications Director controls the system and its equipment from within the Operations Room.

There are a number of pre-set communications plans that configure the communications chain by selecting transmitters, receivers, antennas and internal routing in accordance with operational requirements. With the push of a button a new communications plan can be activated in preparation for a change in mission or situation. Variations to the plan to suit current circumstances can also be rapidly implemented.

The ship's internal communications comprise internal voice communications, main broadcast, wire-free communications, formal and informal messaging, data services and audio-visual entertainment facilities. By using a modular software architecture and software-programmable radios, FICS can be readily adapted to meet future requirements. Consequently it will be able to take advantage of new waveforms without needing new hardware.

Ease of use combined with a high degree of integration and automation all contribute to the reduction of personnel needed to operate the communications system yet allow a quicker response in times of high stress. For instance, the FICS management system controls and monitors the system, performing tasks previously requiring ship's staff. The management system holds information about the antenna environment and performance such as radio path parameters that it predicts from fixed database and real-time channel evaluation techniques. Using this information, it automatically optimises the operating frequencies and on-board asset selection needed to implement the communications plans. An automatic message handling system has also rendered other traditionally manual tasks unnecessary. This high-grade military messaging system automates the reliable distribution and processing of operational messages at all levels of security classification. Based on commercial off-the-shelf equipment developed for its Windows 2000 security enhanced operating system, it provides an interface for the creation, modification and

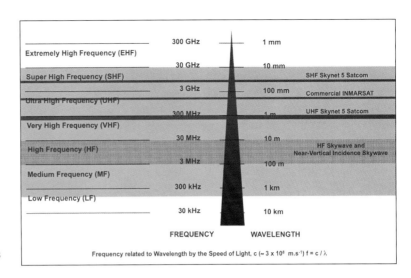

ABOVE **Electro-magnetic spectrum used by warships for communication.**
(Author)

dissemination of messages as well as offering extensive audit and journal services.

A communications transfer system carries communications traffic within the ship. This comprises a number of broadband local area networks employing asynchronous transfer mode and Ethernet technologies. A local area network is dedicated to carrying secure signals.

External terrestrial communications

In order to be able to achieve both global and local communications, warships require transmitters and receivers over a range of frequencies from low (LF) to ultra high (UHF).

For long-range communication there is the high-frequency (HF) system (that also embraces some lower-frequency communication). The HF software defined radios provide a flexible, multi-channel, multi-mode operation and networked capability. Each cabinet includes the radio, embedded modem, an exciter to generate the requisite waveforms and highly linear power amplifiers to boost the signals to levels necessary to achieve global transmission. Each cabinet is a complete transceiver and can operate either within FICS or, in an emergency, independently. It provides voice, data, video, messaging and email services. While predominately operating in the 3MHz to 30MHz HF band, it can also transmit in part of the

JACKSPEAK

Much
telecommunication
and computer
equipment has a
width of 483mm
(19in), allowing
convenient
assembly by
bolting on to
cabinet uprights.
The cabinets are a
neat 600mm wide.
This arrangement
dates back to the
original General
Post Office tele-
communications
equipment of the
1920s, and units
are still described
as '19in Post
Office racks'.

medium frequency (MF) band and can receive
at frequencies down to about 100kHz.

The advantages of software-defined radios
are that they are versatile, programmable and
readily configurable, as well as easily adapted to
future changes in communications technology.

A multi-coupler unit connects the HF radios
to the three 10m whip and two loop antennas.
One antenna is used for the Link-11 tactical
data-link. The system also has new capabilities,
such as automatic link establishment and
automatic repeat request, that greatly improve
communications efficiency and reduce the
number of communications operators needed.

For short-range communications, warships
use VHF maritime and UHF military bands for
ship-to-shore, ship-to-ship and ship-to-air line
of sight communication. Their frequency range
includes VHF civil air traffic control and land
mobile frequencies. The V/UHF software-defined
radio transceivers provide multi-band, multi-mode
communications for voice and data services.

The radios can be used at a fixed frequency.
However, to provide greater security they
incorporate electronic protection measures (the
European supplier's term for the rather clumsy
but normally used term 'electronic counter-
countermeasures'). For instance, they incorporate
SATURN (second generation anti-jam tactical
UHF radio for NATO). This features more
complex fast frequency-hopping than the first
generation (HAVEQUICK), with which, however, it
is compatible. As the name suggests, frequency-
hopping describes very rapid changes in the
frequency of transmission in an apparent random
fashion. The carrier waves can be both amplitude
and frequency modulated.

Because the wavelengths at V/UHF are
smaller than those of HF, and because they do
not require the power for global communications,
both V/UHF antennas and equipment are smaller
than their HF equivalents. Communications data
rates increase with frequency, so the data that
can be passed at these frequencies is much
greater than at HF, albeit over much-reduced
ranges. Most of the antennas are on the
polemast, arranged in sets of four dipole antennas
(facing forward, aft, port and starboard to give
good all-round coverage). There are three sets
arranged vertically and separated by horizontal

Naval high-frequency software-defined radio	
Cabinet dimensions (W x H x D)	600 x 1,900 x 600mm
Cabinet weight	< 1,600kg (dependent on configuration)
Exciter frequency range	1.5 to 30MHz (MF and HF)
Exciter power	500 or 1,000kW
Receiver frequency range	10kHz to 30MHz (LF, MF and HF)

LEFT **External communications
antennas.** *(Author)*

BELOW **Very/ultra-high frequency software-
defined radio transmitter/receiver.** *(Thales)*

1 Commercial Inmarsat.
2 Military satcom (port and starboard).
3 HF near-vertical incidence loops (port
  and starboard).
4 Satellite television receiver.
5 8.75m HF whip.
6 V/UHF polemast.
7 10m HF whip.

Very/ultra-high frequency antennas on polemast.
(Author)

1 JTIDS UHF antenna.
2 Disc screen.
3 Four UHF antennae.
4 Disc screen.
5 Four VHF antennae.
6 Disc screen.
7 Four VHF antennae.
8 Bi-conical dipole UHF antennas (port and starboard).

Naval very/ultra-high frequency transceiver	
Dimensions (W x H x D)	483mm x 177mm x 500mm
Weight	30kg
Transmitter frequency ranges	VHF 118 to 173.975MHz UHF 225 to 399.975MHz
Carrier output	Amplitude modulated – 32W Frequency modulated – 50W
Receiver frequency range	VHF 108 to 173.975MHz UHF 225 to 399.975MHz

ABOVE Foremast showing the port antenna of the satellite communications on-board terminal. *(BAE Systems)*

metallic discs that reduce interaction and mutual interference between the antenna sets. Additional V/UHF antennae have been placed on the superstructure, for instance on the four spars of the main mast. An UHF two-element co-linear array antenna for Link-16 (joint tactical information distribution system) data-link is mounted at the top of the polemast. This omnidirectional antenna operates from 960MHz to 1215MHz.

Military satellite communications

Military satellite communication (satcoms) is used for long-range, high data rate operational communications. Transmissions from the ship to the satellite are retransmitted by the satellite's transponders to ground stations. The ground stations use the satellites and terrestrial links to relay signals globally between headquarters, ships of the fleet and other military assets. Satcoms has the advantage of providing secure, jam-resistant broadband communications with uninterrupted operation under the most adverse weather and sea conditions.

Secure command and support data and voice signals intended for satcoms are passed from FICS45 communications terminals to the ship's two satellite communications on-board terminal (SCOT). Each terminal is connected to a satcoms dish antenna on either side of the foremast. The two dishes ensure all-round coverage. The antennas are fully balanced and are stabilised with a three-axes movement in order to track the communications satellites. The ship's satcoms operate in the super-high frequency (SHF) range but are fitted to receive UHF satcoms equipment.

Satcoms operates with the new constellation of integrated fourth generation Skynet 5 communications satellites, although while Skynet 4

LEFT Detail of satellite communications antenna with radome removed. *(Astrium)*

Skynet 5 hardened military communications satellites	
Dimensions	4.5m x 2.9m x 3.7m
Solar array span	34m
Launch weight	4,700kg
SHF channels	15 (bandwidths from 20MHz to 40MHz)
Transponders	3 x 160W travelling wave tube simplified
UHF channels	9 (bandwidths 5 or 25kHz)
Launch Skynet 5A	11 March 2007; 6.1°E
Launch Skynet 5B	14 November 2007; 52.8°E (25°E December 2012)
Launch Skynet 5C	12 June 2008; 17.8°W
Launch Skynet 5D	19 December 2012; 53°E
Orbit	Geostationary (35,800km above the earth)

satellites remain in service warships can also access them. Enhanced ground station equipment was introduced as part of the Skynet 5 system.

Skynet 5 not only supports operational communications but also welfare communications. This provides all personnel on operations with phone calls and Internet communications to their families at home.

The British Forces Broadcasting Service primarily uses commercial satellites to broadcast ship's television services. However, with equipment known as Television Over Military Satellite it can use Skynet 4 satellites to broadcast special recreational television and news programmes with high image quality. Such broadcasts are provided during the World Cup, for instance.

In the event of failure of the SCOT, a contingency routing facility reallocates ship's priority traffic to Inmarsat commercial maritime satcoms.

RIGHT Fourth-generation Skynet 5 communications satellite. *(Astrium)*

Inmarsat commercial maritime satcoms

Commercial maritime satcoms is now common on merchant vessels, from tankers to cruise liners. It offers a range of communication and safety services, including voice and broadband Internet Protocol data for both vessel operations and for crew and passenger connectivity.

Type 45 destroyers are fitted with the commercial Inmarsat C digital satellite communication system to provide two-way data communications to and from virtually anywhere in the world. The satellite dish used to transmit and receive signals is mounted on the bridge roof. The system is accessed through a Fleet 77 Inmarsat terminal.

Inmarsat can communicate integrated services digital network data, high-quality voice signals, high-quality (3.1kHz) audio signals and other data messages. It can consequently be used for telephony, Internet access, email, weather and chart updates, and for telemedicine. This encoded digital traffic is transmitted in a series of data packets through the Inmarsat C satellite to a Land Earth station that acts as a gateway between the satellite and the message destination. Messages can then be routed to the terrestrial telecommunications network or to other Inmarsat-equipped ships and subscribers. The Inmarsat C system is known as a 'store and forward' messaging system. The Land Earth station stores the data packets and assembles them into a single message that is forwarded to its addressed destination. The Land Earth station automatically reduces transmission errors because if it receives any data packet with errors, a signal is sent back to the terminal requesting the retransmission of those packets until a complete error-free message is received.

The Type 45 destroyers' Inmarsat system fully supports the Global Maritime Distress and Safety System. This is a set of equipment with internationally accepted procedures, and communication protocols that make it easier to rescue distressed ships, boats and aircraft, so increasing safety at sea. The system fitted includes advanced features such as emergency call prioritisation and long-range identification and tracking systems. The Global Maritime Distress and Safety System alerts ships to vessels in distress (including their position) and helps in the coordination of search and rescue.

Internal communications

The internal communications facilities of FICS45 include point-to-point, main broadcast, alarms and intercom communications as well as conferencing facilities. The principal internal communications device is the voice user unit. These units are built into consoles, such as those in the Operations Room and the SCC, or attached to suitable surfaces. FICS45 also has user data terminals that are used to manage the internal and external communications. The ship is amply provided
with these devices and VUUs (which together number more than the permanent ship's complement). The ship also has a number of secure personal computers and laptops that can be connected to the internal network. Authorised operators can be connected through the dial-up strategic communications system to external communications networks for unclassified voice and data communications. The equivalent connections for secure voice and data communications are routed through, and controlled by, the Communications Supervisor's console.

The VUU enables operators to speak to other members of the ship's staff within the ship using both secure and unclassified networks. FICS45 can seamlessly connect to operators on the bridge, the weather deck and flight deck through the wire-free communications system. Even the pilot and navigator in the helicopter on the flight deck may be briefed through the helicopter telebrief interface. The VUU allows operators to change the voice communications channel (internal or external) by touch alone, without having to look up from their primary workstation viewing area.

Access to internal and external communications, as well as to operator consoles for both CMS and PMS, requires a password. The single password identification and authentication system ensures that each operator has a single user name and password for all systems. This avoids the difficulties

Inmarsat commercial communications satellite system	
Dimensions	7.0m x 2.9m x 2.3m
Solar array span	45m
Launch weight	6,000kg
Land Earth stations	40
Network coordination station	One per region to control communications traffic
UHF up-link	1626.5 to 1645.5MHz
UHF down-link	1530.0 to 1545.0MHz
Fleet broadband satellites	Three geostationary (35,800km above the earth)
Launch Inmarsat-4 satellite F1	11 March 2005; Asia-Pacific; 143.5°E
Launch Inmarsat-4 satellite F2	8 November 2005; Europe, Middle East and Africa; 25°E
Launch Inmarsat-4 satellite F3	18 August 2008; Americas; 98°W

experienced by operators of earlier warships who had to remember multiple complex passwords to access several different systems. The passwords ensure that appropriate levels of access are applied to each operator.

As well as the VUU, there are over 300 standard telephones within the ship and a further 50 self-powered telephones for emergency use.

With its link to external communications at sea and in harbour, the communications system gives continuous access to external video teleconferencing facilities and allows ready access to on-shore medical and engineering expertise. Such telecommunications use voice communication supplemented with image and instrument data being exchanged as email attachments.

The internal communications system provides access to CCTV surveillance images at user data terminals in key operational spaces such as the bridge. There are 22 cameras providing

BELOW Officer in ship control centre voice user unit.
(Crown Copyright, 2013 PO(Phot) Paul Punter)

S2 voice user unit characteristics	
Integrated services digital network ports	1 or 2
Simultaneous communications	16
External communications	32 radio circuits
Internal communications	256 circuits
Security	Embedded red/black separation Plain/encrypted indicator
Ethernet ports	1 x 100Mbps
Dimensions (W x H x D)	142mm x 267mm x 120mm
Weight	3kg
Power supply	20W at 24–48V DC

weather-deck and flight-deck coverage to ensure the ship's safety and security. The PMS uses additional CCTV cameras for surveillance of the machinery spaces.

Ship's recreational equipment

The ship's recreational equipment (formerly the 'sound reproduction equipment') supplies television entertainment and a range of audio-visual devices. It now includes iPods, with charging facilities and docking stations in mess decks. The communicators' unofficial job of yesteryear as ship's postman has been exchanged for individual external email access. Daily orders are also now promulgated by intranet rather than paper.

The British Forces Broadcasting Service broadcasts television entertainment to ships of the fleet by the Commercial Stabilised Satellite Television System operated and maintained by

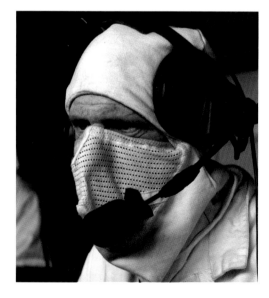

RIGHT Member of HMS *Diamond*'s bridge team wearing infrared communication mobile unit headset over anti-flash gear.
(Crown Copyright, 2011 PO(Phot) Paul Punter)

the MoD. The television system also has more serious applications, such as the delivery of training material and ship's company briefings. A Television Receive Only stabilised satellite dish is mounted on the aft side of the funnel for television reception. This antenna is stabilised on three axes in order to track the selected satellite. When in harbour, the ship is connected to terrestrial systems to receive television broadcasts.

Infrared communications

Military infrared communications is a digitally encoded system that allows working groups of ship's staff to remain in contact wherever they are. It is a secure network and meets TEMPEST requirements. The system is also used by operators in the noisy environments of the flight deck and machinery spaces. Such roaming communication is also available for selected operators with duties on the bridge, in the Operations Room and for members of damage control parties. Operators have a communication mobile unit comprising a headset and belt-mounted battery pack. It offers the user total freedom of movement while providing effective two-way voice communications. Every headset allows communication with other mobile users or operators at any position within the ship. Operators with enhanced equipment can also access external communications.

Headsets give mobile users clear two-way (duplex) voice communications and, because it is a multi-channel system, different groups of operators can maintain independent communications even when they are working within the same area of the ship. The infrared system may be used in areas where there are high levels of electro-magnetic interference (such as machinery spaces and the enclosed quarterdeck), as it is immune to severe energy pulses. This gives it a significant advantage over traditional radio or inductive loop systems that were sensitive to interference. The headsets are of two types — noise-attenuating headsets for use when working in areas where high acoustic noise levels exist, and lightweight versions for other spaces. Both kinds have noise-cancelling microphones to reduce the background noise superimposed on the user's voice when speaking.

A number of base stations are mounted in convenient locations about the ship and provide the interface with the ship's communication system. The low-level infrared eliminates ocular hazards while providing exceptional coverage with multi-channel capability. The ability to employ virtually unlimited infrared antennas from each base station ensures communication with many users over areas of up to 100m². As the range is predictable it can be restricted to point-to-point communications, making infrared the ideal medium for secure and sensitive communications. However, there must be an uninterrupted line of sight between the base station antennas and the transceiver unit on the top of each user's headset. Every base station antenna can provide coverage over more than 90°, with a range of up to 10m. Each antenna is mounted on a bracket to ensure that the antenna can be pointed in the most appropriate direction. The headset has a 360° field of view. By connecting a control cable between the two base stations it is possible to operate two systems in the same area, with one base station nominated as the 'master'. This allows two totally independent systems to be used within the same infrared environment.

Medium-frequency sonar (MFS) Type 2091

MFS is mounted in the destroyer's bow dome. The dome, which is filled with seawater when the sonar is operational, incorporates internal baffles to reduce both noise transmissions from astern and internal reflections within the dome. The MFS emlts pulses to actively detect and identify underwater threats such as submarines, torpedoes or mines. It automatically processes the returned pulses to localise threats. While it can also operate passively by analysing the noise emanating from potential targets, the lack of range information yielded by passive detection means that tracks have to be analysed and confirmed manually.

The sonar within the dome is a cylindrical array of 36 vertical staves that provide 360° coverage. Each stave comprises 10 transducers. For mine hunting only the transducers of the forward 7 staves are used.

For communications with submarines, an omnidirectional underwater telephone is used. This transmits and receives voice messages using underwater acoustic radiation, and operates at NATO-allocated frequencies of 8kHz to 42kHz. The underwater telephone is blanked when the MFS emits a pulse.

Meteorological and oceanographic (METOC) system

METOC is a suite of individual environmental sensors and receivers whose data is integrated and displayed on a dedicated workstation in the chartroom located aft of the bridge. The system automatically captures data about wind and air as well as automatically receiving satellite image and weatherfax data. It also collects and processes data from manually launched bathythermograph probes and from upper air sounding system radio-sondes. The METOC workstation collates, displays and distributes environmental data to the Type 45 combat system and other users by the data transfer system. The information is thus available to operators at workstations of the navigation system, CMS, secondary data display system and PMS. METOC also automatically compiles routine weather reports and manually exchanges such reports with other units and shore stations.

LEFT Medium-frequency sonar dome on cradle for installation and removal. *(Ultra Electronics)*

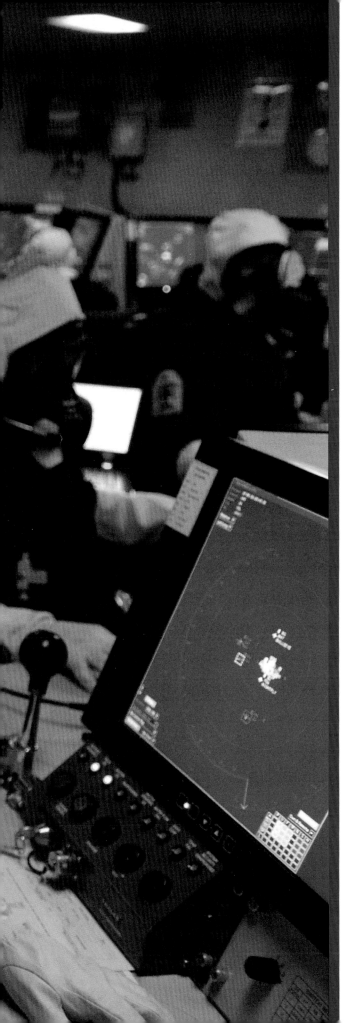

Chapter Four

The operation of Type 45 Destroyers

In an era of almost continuous political tension, the Type 45 destroyers represent a persuasive deterrent against military escalation. However, if necessary they are powerful enough to fully engage in aggressive actions. They not only have the capability to attack hostile missiles and aircraft but also ships, submarines and land targets.

OPPOSITE During HMS *Daring*'s nine-month deployment of 2013–14, officers in the operations room don gas masks and anti-flash gear for a simulated attack involving chemical warfare. *(Crown Copyright, 2014 LA(Phot) Keith Morgan)*

113

Type 45 destroyers are primarily intended to undertake one of the most challenging roles of naval warfare – to defend a naval task group against air attack. One such group might be a Strike Group led by an aircraft carrier and another could be an Amphibious Task Group whose objective is to land forces on enemy territory. Both groups contain a mix of warships, high-value units, mission essential units and their auxiliaries. In the longer term, Type 45 destroyers are intended to provide force protection to groups led by the new HMS *Queen Elizabeth* Class aircraft carriers that are due to enter service in 2020.

The Type 45 destroyers' Sea Viper system is capable of attacking a variety of air targets at a range of up to 100km, and can be visualised as projecting a protective umbrella over the area of operations of the force. The destroyers can engage sophisticated missiles such as those that have adopted steep-diving flight profiles to avoid detection, while also protecting against sea-skimming anti-ship missiles that fly a few metres above the sea's surface and appear suddenly over the horizon.

When involved with amphibious operations the destroyers' Sea Viper systems will provide defence for the amphibious warships in transit and during the landing. As the assault progresses, and the force approaches the landing site, the destroyers' air cover will extend to land forces as well as vessels in the littoral. Their sensors enable the destroyers to develop a high-quality tactical picture, and their sophisticated communications equipment allows them to share this situational awareness with friendly forces at sea and on land.

Apart from Sea Viper, Type 45 destroyers have a flexible suite of weapons and sensors that includes MCG for shore bombardment and SCGs that can be used in counter-piracy and anti-smuggling operations. These enable the destroyers to be deployed on a variety of military tasks and to conduct operations in a wide range of scenarios. They are therefore well able to meet a secondary requirement – the need to provide security at sea. This encompasses peacekeeping in times of heightened tension, making sure the ocean sea routes are safe for commercial shipping, preventing international crimes and providing assistance in times of political or natural emergencies. If they are to be prepared for these operational tasks anywhere in the world, however, the ships' companies must regularly take part in realistic exercises in a range of environments.

Action stations

When an attack is imminent or deemed probable, a warship's company is called to action stations and the ship is configured to ensure that it is robust in the event of damage being inflicted. The highest state of readiness, Zulu Alpha (or ZA), requires that the greatest watertight and gastight integrity is achieved. The ship's citadel is broadly the superstructure and all those compartments immediately below it. This central section of the ship is subdivided into four zones that, in ZA state, form four sealed gastight sections by closing all gastight doorways. All hatches and openings are closed to prevent the spread of flooding or fire. The ship's service machinery is brought on line and configured in such a way that each zone may have its own autonomous services. Damage to one zone will not then affect adjacent zones. Likewise the IEPS is divided into a 'four island' configuration that provides maximum robustness to failure and flexibility of operation. The busbar ties of both 4.16kV switchboards are opened so that the GTAs supply only the propulsion systems and the 440V ship's service switchboards are supplied solely by the diesel alternators.

No warship is completely airtight, and the citadel's gastight integrity can be compromised by holes produced by action damage, and by personnel accessing the weather deck through airlocks. Therefore the ship's citadel is maintained at a positive pressure so that leaking air moves out from the citadel, thus preventing the penetration of CBRN agents.

With the ship sealed, the ventilation system recirculates the air within the ship. To provide fresh air for the ship's complement and to replace any air leaking from the citadel, additional air is drawn into the ship only through special filters that remove all potential contaminants. The down-takes continue to supply air to the sealed gas turbine and diesel engine enclosures, but the down-take air inlets to the machinery spaces are closed. Cooling coils supplied with CW are then employed to extract heat from machinery spaces.

To further protect the ship from CBRN agents, the pre-wetting system is started, veiling the ship in seawater mist to prevent contaminants from settling on and adhering to the weather decks. This mist is produced by sprayers, nozzles and drenchers sited and angled to ensure the whole substructure and weather deck are covered (with the exception of air intakes for ventilation and machinery). To spread the pre-wetting mist over the ship in calm weather, the ship's stabilisers – normally used to reduce roll in heavy weather – can be used in opposition to generate a slight roll.

Under gastight conditions ship's personnel only venture on to the potentially contaminated weather deck if they are wearing full CBRN protection suits and respirators. They must exit the ship through one of the airlocks to prevent harmful agents penetrating the citadel boundary.

Personnel may only re-enter through a cleansing station that allows them to remove any contamination from their suits. The door to the cleansing station allows personnel to enter an airlock that is also a stripping area. Once the door to the weather deck has been closed they may remove all contaminated clothing and equipment and then open the interior door to a second airlock. Only when the door to the stripping area is closed may personnel open the next door and move into an area where they shower to remove any residual contamination. Once this is done they may enter the final airlock to don clean uniforms and enter the ship. The key to the process is that each door to the next space is only opened once the

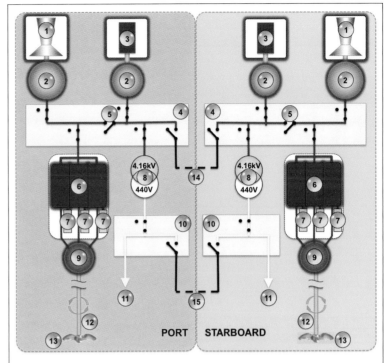

1 Gas turbine.	**9** Propulsion motor.
2 Alternator.	**10** 440V switchboard.
3 Diesel.	**11** Ship's service supply 440V, three-
4 4.16kV switchboard.	phase, 60Hz.
5 Busbar tie.	**12** Propeller shaft.
6 Converter.	**13** Propeller.
7 Dynamic breaking resistors.	**14** 4.16kV interconnector.
8 Ship's service transformer 2.5MVA.	**15** 440V interconnector.

ABOVE Integrated electrical propulsion system single line diagram showing the 'four island' configuration (filters omitted for simplicity). *(Author from General Electric Company information)*

BELOW LEFT Sailors wearing chemical, biological, radiological and nuclear protection suits and respirators. *(Crown Copyright, 2005 POA(Phot) Mick Storey)*

BELOW RIGHT Port 01-Deck watertight and gastight entrance to the citadel through an airlock and cleansing station under the port small-calibre gun platform. *(Airfix)*

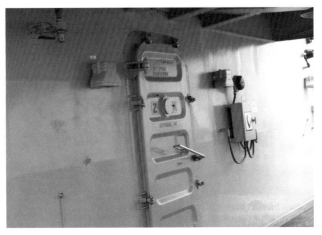

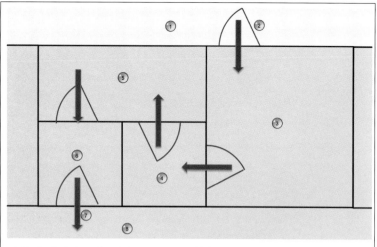

1 Contaminated weather deck.
2 Entrance to cleansing station.
3 Stripping area.
4 Airlock.
5 Cleansing station.
6 Airlock and dressing area.
7 Exit from cleansing station.
8 Ship's citadel.

ABOVE Plan of typical cleansing station. *(Author)*

The PMS is linked to the following CBRN warning systems that provide a continuous operational monitoring system for contamination both within the ship and in the external air and seawater:

■ Ship's installed chemical agent detection system to monitor for chemical agents such as nerve gases.
■ Ship's maritime biological detection system to monitor for biological agents.
■ Ship's installed radiological detection system to monitor direct, induced or residual nuclear radiation.

At Action Stations most galley and logistics personnel are assigned operational duties such as assisting the medical staff with first aid. They also support the damage control parties distributed about the ship to fight fires, stem floods and appraise the command team of the developing operational situation.

previous door has been closed. This, combined with the pressurised air flowing from the ship towards the weather deck opening, ensures that contaminants do not enter the ship.

When tackling fires members of the damage control parties wear self-contained breathing apparatus, helmets and protective clothing.

It is vital to determine the source of fires, and for this purpose firefighters are equipped with thermal imaging cameras. These lightweight hand-held devices allow firefighters to locate hot areas and the seat of the fire and so concentrate their hoses on the source. The cameras can operate in complete darkness and conditions of zero visibility caused by smoke. They also allow personnel to identify and rescue casualties as well as detecting hot bulkheads that indicate fires in adjacent compartments.

RIGHT Chef assists HMS *Dauntless* medical team by providing emergency first aid as part of a training exercise. *(Crown Copyright, 2012 LA(Phot) Nicola Wilson)*

RIGHT HMS *Dauntless*'s firefighters wearing self-contained breathing apparatus, helmets and protective clothing. *(Crown Copyright, 2012 LA(Phot) Nicola Wilson)*

FAR RIGHT Firefighter using thermal imaging camera. *(Crown Copyright, 2012 LA(Phot) Ben Sutton)*

Anti-air warfare (AAW)

The key to successful AAW is defence in depth. This is the ability to initially engage hostile targets at the greatest range possible and complement this with several closer-range layers of defence. Area air defence missiles engage the threats at long range, with local area air defence missiles and point defence weapons tackling any hostile targets that avoid the outer layer or suddenly appear at shorter range.

Although Sea Viper allows Type 45 destroyers to operate totally independently of other forces, their effectiveness is greatly enhanced by knowledge of the wider picture. Aircraft, because of their height, are well placed to deliver this information. Maritime patrol aircraft were primarily intended to deliver dedicated maritime support to ASW task forces, but they were also a source of intelligence, surveillance, targeting, acquisition and reconnaissance information for naval forces. They were well placed to identify threats close to the surface that are beyond the destroyers' horizon, and to alert the warships to potential attacks. This role is partially filled by airborne warning and control system (AWACS) aircraft that provide information about the long-range air picture to all forces in a theatre of war.

The RAF's E-3D Sentry Airborne Early Warning Aircraft or, in joint operations, the USAF E-3 Sentry AWACS, fulfil this role. A limitation of these aircraft is that they have to operate from friendly airbases and, should there be no bases near the area of operations, their time on task is limited. As was discovered in the Falklands conflict in 1982, it is essential to have organic airborne early warning within the fleet, so Sea King helicopters were rapidly fitted with AWACS equipment. The latest version of

this system is the Sea King ASaC7, introduced in 2002. It has a new mission system based around the improved Searchwater 2000AEW radar that can simultaneously track, if necessary, about 400 targets. The helicopter's main role is the detection of low-flying aircraft whose position and characteristics are communicated to the naval force by the integrated Link-16 data-link. Data-links are also essential to obtain information from other ships, particularly ASW warships (such as the Type 23 frigates) that operate at the edges of the force and might be the first to receive warning of low-level attacks.

When a naval group includes aircraft carriers, their aircraft fly combat air patrols to give advanced warning of attack and to provide an additional means of prosecuting hostile aircraft before they can launch their missiles. Such aircraft will not be available to the RN until the HMS *Queen Elizabeth* Class carriers receive F35B Lightning II fighter/bombers. Meanwhile, the group will have to rely on fighter aircraft flown from other nations' carriers in the group and, where possible, land-based aircraft.

ABOVE RAF E-3D Sentry Airborne Early Warning Aircraft. *(Steve Wright)*

BELOW Sea King ASaC7 airborne surveillance and control helicopter with Searchwater 2000AEW radar. *(Crown Copyright, 2005 POA(Phot) Mick Storey)*

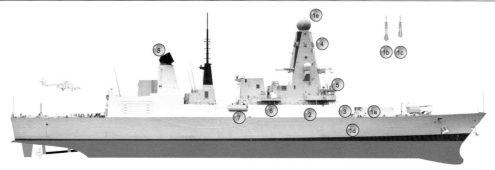

1 Sea Viper anti-air warfare system comprising:
  a Sylver A-50 launcher.
  b Aster-30 missiles.
  c Aster-15 missiles.
  d Sea Viper local command and control.
  e Sampson multifunction radar Type 1045.
2 Combat management system.
3 Outfit DLH launchers (port and starboard).

4 Outfit UAT radar electronic surveillance measures.
5 Electro-optic gunfire control system (port and starboard).
6 Outfit DLF(3) Seagnat launchers.
7 20mm Block 1B Phalanx close-in weapons system (port and starboard).
8 Long-range radar Type 1046.

As the weapon providing AAW defence, Sea Viper can counter hostile targets from any angle and saturation attacks that require simultaneous engagement of multiple targets. It can destroy high-speed missiles launched by helicopters and aircraft and defeat a sudden attack of sea-skimming missiles fired by a submarine, surface ship or aircraft. Despite the difficulties experienced by radars in the littoral environment, Sea Viper's Sampson MFR is able to search for and detect targets flying over land by performing different types of search pattern in conjunction with its other tasks. It is complemented by electronic support measures that can detect the radars of missiles and aircraft and so provide a warning of hostile targets as well as the direction of attack.

BELOW **Commanding Officer at his multifunction console in the operations room with the Anti-Air Warfare Officer on his left.** *(Crown Copyright, 2011 PO(Phot) Paul Punter)*

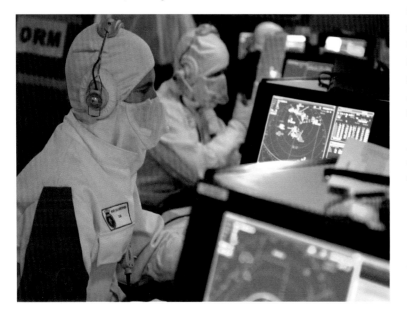

The CMS's software ensures that the data from all sensors is fused. Consequently, the same physical object seen by more than one sensor is reported only once and is accompanied by the best available composite information. Data from the IFF equipment is also used to determine which tracks are friendly. Any potential threats are passed to Sampson MFR, which will then concentrate on that track in order to confirm the plot information. Sea Viper undertakes a threat evaluation using complex software-based logic, running on a high-speed processing platform. The importance of the track is then compared to all other tracks being monitored. Sampson MFR tracks the most dangerous threats in a dedicated mode that increases the time that the Sampson MFR dwells on serious targets. All data relating to air targets is coordinated at the Air Picture Controller's console in the Operations Room. Serious threats will prompt weapon assignment and a launch command, automatically selecting Aster-30 missiles for long-range engagements and Aster-15 for shorter ones.

The situation is closely monitored by the Anti-Air Warfare Officer and the Principal Warfare Officer, who have consoles that flank the Commanding Officer's console in the Operations Room. The Sea Viper Controller, immediately behind them, will be preparing to engage the most threatening hostile targets. To provide a rapid reaction the system is highly automated, although the decision to permit firing remains the responsibility of the ship's officers.

The Sea Viper command and control system

optimises the response to the attack from hostile targets. If the command team approves an engagement then the Sea Viper's Aster missiles will be launched. Prior to launch the selected missiles in their Sylver launchers are relayed initialisation data about the optimum predicted trajectory to intercept the target, the target's position and the jamming environment. Meanwhile, the doors covering those missiles' canisters flip open. Seconds later the missile's booster fires, creating sufficient pressure to break the frangible cover of the missile's canister. As the missile ascends its efflux is directed to a plenum chamber at the base of the launcher and then up a long duct between the two rows of missiles, erupting as a plume of bright orange flame. The Aster missiles can reach Mach 4.5 in about two seconds.

The serious nature of the threat may demand the firing of a salvo of missiles to maximise the probability of a kill. With the first missile in flight and arcing away in a plume of smoke, a second missile can follow a few seconds later.

Once the Aster missile has reached a sufficient height, the booster's thrust vector control nozzles turn it in the direction of the target as indicated by the autopilot's inertial navigation system. During this period its computers shape its trajectory to reduce the effects of jamming and to optimise the angle of approach to the target. The booster accelerates the Aster missiles, with the larger booster of the Aster-30 burning for longer than that of the Aster-15, giving it greater speed and enabling it to engage higher targets at a longer range. The booster is not joined to the Dart section of Aster so the booster falls away naturally once its fuel is exhausted. The Dart's motor then fires to sustain the approach to its target. Throughout the engagement the Sampson MFR tracks both the Aster and the target's manoeuvres. It sends further data to the Dart by a radar frequency up-link to allow it to correct its course towards the ideal intercept position.

As the Aster Dart approaches the target it switches on its active radar seeker that controls the final approach, operating even in severe electronic countermeasures environments. AAW missiles engage crossing targets that may be aimed at other vessels in the naval force rather than targets coming straight towards the ship.

ABOVE Sequence of Aster missile leaving the Sylver launcher: (a) frangible cover opening under the influence of blast pressure from missile; (b) efflux exiting from chimney; (c) missile emerging; (d) missile leaving launcher. *(Direction Générale de l'Armement).*

LEFT Aster-30 missile fired from HMS *Daring*. *(MBDA UK)*

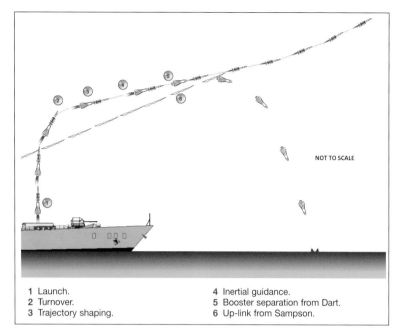

1 Launch.
2 Turnover.
3 Trajectory shaping.
4 Inertial guidance.
5 Booster separation from Dart.
6 Up-link from Sampson.

ABOVE Diagram of the initial phase of an Aster missile firing. *(Author)*

To achieve this, the missile follows a trajectory that aims ahead of the target, as continually aiming for the target will be ineffective. Generically, such a trajectory is termed proportional navigation. Capable of speeds of over 1,500m/sec (Mach 4.5), the Aster Darts are extremely agile. To combat last-minute manoeuvres of the target and ensure that the targets do not evade them, the missile's Dart employs two unique control systems. These are termed PIF (*pilotage d'interception en force* – interception thrust control) and PAF (*pilotage aérodynamique fort* – powerful aerodynamic control). PIF relies on four pairs of vectored thrusters on the side of the Dart that provide a short burst of efflux with a force of 12g. This results in a sideways 'hop', allowing it to overcome even the most evasive dogleg manoeuvres by the target. The second technique, PAF, is an enhanced version of conventional manoeuvring, using aerodynamic control surfaces.

Together they enable the Dart to pursue the target in this terminal phase with turns of up to 60g – making it more than six times more manoeuvrable than the latest fighter aircraft.

These manoeuvres are intended to steer the Dart to an optimum intercept point close to the target. When the electro-magnetic proximity fuze detects the target it detonates the Dart's fragmentation warhead. This produces a cone of fast-moving metal fragments concentrated in the direction of the target and peppering it with damage. Interception does not require the Dart to physically hit the target, and, although the Aster Dart will often obliterate the target, it is only necessary for it to disable it or knock it off course. The final task of the Sampson MFR during the engagement is to assess whether the target has been eliminated as a threat or if a further engagement is necessary.

In normal operation, Sea Viper is controlled from the Operations Room using the ship's CMS, the system that collates all the information gathered by all the ship's sensors and data-links. However, in an emergency the Sea Viper command and control main processor unit can provide many of the functions normally undertaken by the CMS. It can be operated from a pair of emergency consoles (identical to those in the Operations Room) located close to the launcher. Sampson MFR can provide all the data needed over a direct link and this can be supplemented by LRR data if available.

1 Aster Dart.
2 Hostile target.
3 Inertial guidance.
4 Dart's radar begins search.
5 Dart's radar acquires target.
6 Proportional navigation engaged.
7 *Pilotage d'interception en force* (PIF).
8 *Pilotage aérodynamique fort* (PAF).
9 Proximity fuze detonates warhead and destroys target.

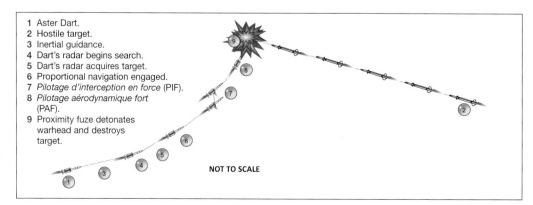

RIGHT Diagram of Aster Dart homing sequence. *(Author)*

With Aster-30 and shorter-range Aster-15 missiles, Type 45 destroyers offer the group two main layers of defence against threats targeted at vessels of the group: medium-range air defence and local area air defence. The former, provided by Aster-30 missiles, defends against hostile aircraft and their anti-ship missiles out to a range of 100km. Local area defence, supplied by Aster-15 missiles, protects the group from any missiles not destroyed by the Aster-30 shield. An equally important local area defence role is to protect the force from pop-up or late unmasking missile attacks launched by submarines or by ships and helicopters over the horizon. In the littoral, such attacks may also come from land-based launchers and low-flying aircraft taking advantage of the terrain to mask their approach. The hostile missiles are also stealthy and highly manoeuvrable so difficult to engage. In order to be effective Aster-15 needs sufficient warning. The higher the main radar is located then the further away (and earlier) it can detect low-altitude threats. The Sampson MFR on the top of the foremast has a theoretical radar horizon of between 30km and 50km (depending on the conditions and the height of the hostile missile). Even so, supersonic missiles travelling from this distance can strike a ship in the group in less than 45 seconds.

Should any hostile missiles or aircraft manage to penetrate these outer layers of defence, most ships of the group have some self-defence capability. Whereas the Aster missiles can intercept missiles on a crossing trajectory and so protect other ships, the two Phalanx guns (assisted by the SCGs against aircraft) are for self-defence. The Phalanx Block 1B CIWS is a quick-reaction defence system that provides final defence against incoming

air targets. It is a standalone weapon system with its own radars and electro-optical sensors that automatically search for, detect, track and evaluate potential threats. It automatically engages high-speed, low-level threats that penetrate the ship's primary defences. Having engaged a target it subsequently assesses the need to re-engage. With its high rate of fire, it aims to throw up a focused, impenetrable wall of fire between the threat and the warship.

Electronic warfare decoys

D ecoys provide soft-kill defence against missiles and augment the self-defence guns. Rather than physically destroying the threat like the ship's missiles and guns, soft-kill weapons aim to deceive incoming missiles by presenting alternatives for them to target, thereby confusing their homing electronics.

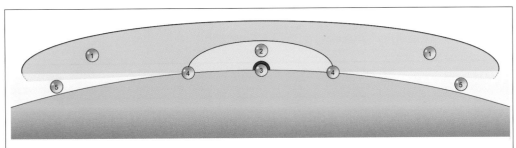

1 Medium-range area defence region (Aster-30).
2 Local area defence region (Aster-15).
3 Self-defence region (Phalanx).
4 Radar horizon for sea-skimming missile.
5 Area beyond the ship's horizon.

Outfit DLH(2) decoy characteristics				
	Mk251	**Mk214**	**Mk216 Mod 1**	**Mk245**
Round	Active decoy	Seduction chaff	Distraction chaff	Mid- and long-wave infrared
Diameter	130mm	130mm	130mm	130mm
Length	1.70m	1.22m	1.22m	1.20m
Weight	28kg	23kg	25kg	22kg
Author/photos Chemring				

Outfit DLH's Seagnat launcher can fire four types of decoy round:

- Mk251 active decoy round.
- Mk216 distraction chaff round.
- Mk214 seduction chaff round.
- Mk245 infrared round.

Chaff contains metal-coated filaments whose radar return emulates that of a ship. Chaff decoys are fired into the air, where they explode at a preselected position, dispensing chaff clouds to confuse the enemy's surveillance radar by presenting multiple false targets. While the chaff clouds will eventually disperse, they only need to present alternative targets to the missile for the brief period of its homing phase. The major reason for reducing the radar cross-section of Type 45 destroyers is not to meet the unachievable target of making the ship undetectable, but rather to ensure that the ship's radar return is comparable to that of the expendable decoys, so fooling the incoming missiles that the chaff cloud is their intended target.

The infrared decoy is a flare that counters heat-seeking missiles by producing emissions in both the mid-wavelength and long-wavelength infrared sensor regions. Greater emissions are produced in the higher band, as this typifies a ship's infrared signature. This decoy provides an alternative target for heat-seeking missiles.

The Mk216 distraction round is the first to be deployed from the Seagnat launcher. When it is about 1.5km from the warship, a drogue chute deploys to slow the round. The round slowly descends beneath the chute, with pyrotechnic charges dispensing three chaff payloads in turn. This technique is effective if the hostile missiles have not yet acquired and locked on to their target. If their radar homing-head has locked on to the ship, then the active decoy round is deployed in order to confuse the missile, ensuring that it searches again for a target and, this time, acquires the chaff cloud.

The cartridge round CCM216 Mk1 Type 1 will supersede the Mk216 Mod 1. It deploys a single chaff payload out to 2km. This range, and its cloud height, can be preselected and are

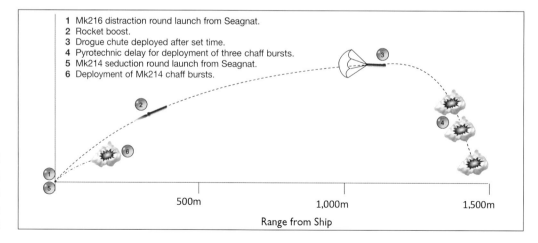

1 Mk216 distraction round launch from Seagnat.
2 Rocket boost.
3 Drogue chute deployed after set time.
4 Pyrotechnic delay for deployment of three chaff bursts.
5 Mk214 seduction round launch from Seagnat.
6 Deployment of Mk214 chaff bursts.

500m   1,000m   1,500m

Range from Ship

RIGHT Deployment of Mk216 distraction and Mk214 seduction rounds. *(Author from Chemring information)*

NOT TO SCALE

LEFT Deployment of Mk216 distraction round. *(Author)*

independent of ship's roll that affects the firing angle and round trajectory of existing decoys.

The new Mk251 active decoy round provides a more sophisticated response to counter radar-homing anti-ship missiles, even those equipped with radar seekers that only switch on as they get close to the ship. This off-board electronic countermeasures decoy system detects and locates the I/J-band radar seekers of incoming anti-ship missiles and then disrupts ('jams') the signal of even the most sophisticated missiles. Earlier generations of jammer generally required the electrical and computing power that could only be provided by the ship. Unfortunately, hostile missiles could switch to a 'home on jam' mode and use the jamming signal as a beacon to steer it to the ship. Thanks to lighter, cheaper and more efficient electronics, the off-board Mk251 beams its signal towards the threat from a position well away from the ship.

The interface between the ship's combat system and the Mk251 in the Seagnat launcher is a fire control unit that automatically or semi-automatically activates the firing. It employs a microprocessor to select the optimum launcher, to programme the correct jamming technique, to choose the best deployment position and to initiate the firing sequence.

If the ship's combat system detects an incoming threat, the threat's identification profile and a control command are downloaded to the selected Mk251 round. When fired from its Seagnat launcher, its inbuilt low-acceleration rocket projects the round about 500m. This distance allows a rapid deployment yet is

sufficiently far from the ship to be effective. The Mk251 round has a two-stage system: a parachute first slows the round at a pre-programmed distance from the ship before a parawing deploys. The programmable electronic payload descends slowly to the sea beneath the parawing and can quickly detect, identify and track threats to the ship. Within a few seconds from the selection of the round, the payload can generate and transmit a signal to counter each specific threat to divert it from the ship. This signal comprises unique deception or jamming waveforms generated using a digital radiofrequency memory loop and software control. These signals, amplified by a travelling wave tube amplifier are highly directional, so the round is able to concentrate this power to defeat the threat. The round can simultaneously handle multiple threats and can continue to do so for the time (about 180sec) that it is held aloft on its parawing.

Like most on-board electronic counter-measures, it is reported that the Mk251 off-board round can use the 'range gate pull-off' technique against homing missiles. This disrupts a missile that is locked on to the ship, forcing it to search again for the target with the intent that it now acquires a distraction round deployed earlier. To employ the range gate pull-off technique, the Mk251 round transmits a radar pulse that emulates the return that the hostile missile receives from the ship. Initially these pulses are returned at about the same time as the ship's return. These false returns will lie within the missile's range gate, a span of ranges bracketing the detected ship. Having acquired and locked

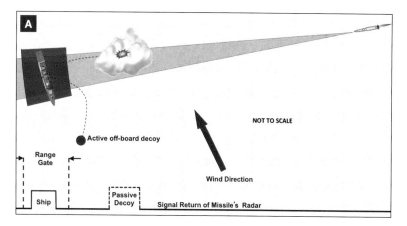

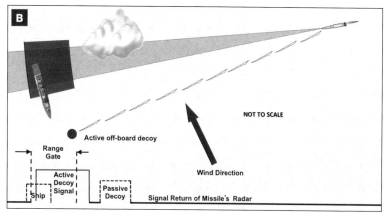

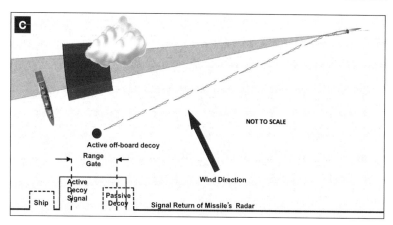

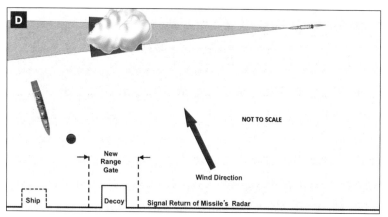

on to its target the missile's electronics will only process signals at about the same range as the ship (ie within a range gate) in order that it cannot be swamped by spurious signals.

Subsequent returns are successfully delayed so that the range gate moves slowly and progressively away from the correct range of the ship, and closer to the range of a decoy. The range gate is thereby pulled off its original ship target by progressively 'walking off'. When this is achieved the jammer is turned off so that the missile no longer receives a return within its range gate. The missile will then search for a new target, with a high probability of locking on to a chaff cloud.

If the missile is not lured by the Mk216 distraction round then the Mk214 seduction round forms the next line of defence. This is also deployed if the threat appears suddenly and there is insufficient time for distraction modes to be employed. Outfit DLH automatically deploys the chaff between the ship and the missile within a matter of seconds.

When a hostile missile is close to the ship its radar will see the ship and the chaff as a single entity and aim for the centre of the combined radar return (the centroid). With the movement of the ship and of the chaff cloud being carried by the wind, the centroid will move in the direction of the chaff cloud. The missile, following the centroid, will then transfer its allegiance to the chaff cloud and be seduced away from the ship as a target.

Mk214 seduction rounds are usually deployed with Mk245 infrared rounds in case the hostile missile has alternative or dual-sensor homing modes. The round incorporates five sequential, airburst sub-munitions each of which, deployed in turn, is a flare emulating a warship's infrared signature.

Chaff clouds are affected by weather conditions. Moderate breezes will not disperse the clouds rapidly but will alter their position. This movement may assist in the centroid mode where the ship and cloud must move apart

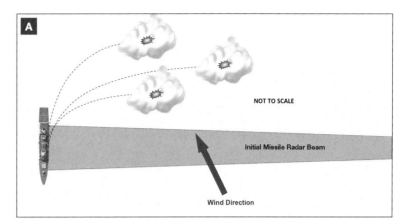

RIGHT **Operation of seduction round:**
(a) deployment; (b) threat successfully decoyed.
(Author)

swiftly. Strong winds will tend to disperse the cloud through turbulence and reduce the time when the cloud is effective. This will enable hostile radars to distinguish chaff unless further clouds are established in approximately the same position. This is difficult in strong winds.

In addition to the Outfit DLH aerial decoys, Type 45 destroyers are also fitted with Outfit DLF(3) passive advanced inflatable radar decoy, an expendable floating decoy. Its operation is fully automatic and it is rapidly ejected from its launch tube by compressed air from an attached gas cylinder. As it falls towards the sea a lanyard coupling the launcher to the decoy activates the decoy's internal gas system, inflating it within seconds. A second lanyard retains the decoy until it is fully inflated. After a short delay line cutters sever this tether, allowing the decoy to float freely along the side of the ship. The nylon structure supports an array of corner reflectors made from radar-reflecting net that replicates the radar return of the ship. It is

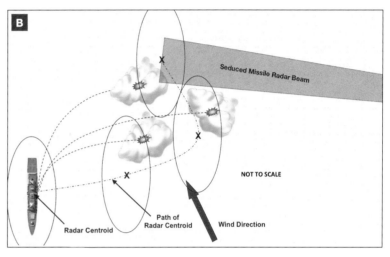

LEFT **HMS** *Dragon* **fires decoys off Portland for the first time during trials, 12 March 2012: (a) first decoy having bloomed; (b) firing off third round.** *(Crown Copyright, 2012)*

JACKSPEAK

The large inflatable decoy DLF (overleaf) was nicknamed 'Rubber Duck'; the later version, DLF(3) is known as 'Rubber Duck successor'.

used in both confusion and seduction modes as an alternative target for the hostile missile. Several hours after deployment, an automatic mechanical cutter deflates the decoy.

Amphibious warfare

Amphibious warfare uses a task force of warships to project military power ashore. Type 45 destroyers are a vital component of an amphibious task force, providing protection from air attack to the assault ships, helicopter carriers and other vessels of the force and generally supporting joint operations. They can transport and insert an Embarked Military Force of up to 60 that can swell the number of troops available for the landing. The destroyers are able to act as a forward operating base for 14 HQ staff, allowing them to plan and execute operations by an Embarked Military Force. This facility increases the range of maritime and joint operations that can be carried out, including power projection against land targets, support of joint operations and the insertion of Special Forces.

The Type 45 destroyer's MCG can provide naval gunfire support to amphibious landings and other operations that require shore bombardment.

During the landing itself, the destroyers' air defence provides protection against enemy aircraft and missiles in areas encompassing landing craft ferrying men and materials ashore, the beachhead and well inland. The destroyers' large flight decks allow Chinook helicopters to land and so transport the embarked troops ashore.

During conflicts, especially amphibious operations, casualties can be evacuated to the destroyers' Role 1 Medical Treatment

ABOVE Captain Robinson, Commanding Officer of HMS *Daring*, and other officers of Combined Task Force 150 in one of the planning rooms. *(Crown Copyright, 2012 LA(Phot) Keith Morgan)*

RIGHT Medium-calibre gun firing. *(BAE Systems)*

Helicopter loads			
	Lynx Mk8	**Merlin HC Mk3**	**Chinook**
Cargo area		6.5m x 2.3m	2.3m x 9.3m
Passengers			
Normal	5	24 seated	33 seated
Gun on rear ramp		16 seated	
Troop-carrying	8 equipped	27 equipped	33 equipped
High density	9 troops	40 troops	55 troops
Stretchers	6	16	24
Carried equipment	None	2 Land Rovers	None
External hook	1 (1.4 tonnes)	1 (2.5 tonnes)	3
Load	1.5 tonnes overall	5.4 tonnes overall	10 tonnes overall
Note: The naval Merlin HM1 can only carry 8 troops or 4 stretchers even with its sonar removed.			

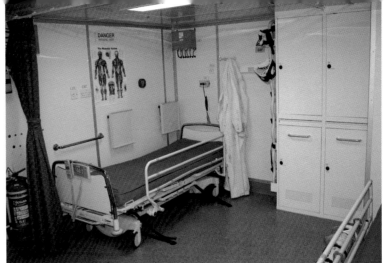

ABOVE Senior officer talking to HMS *Daring*'s ship's surgeon and other medical staff in the sickbay. The adjacent ward can be seen in the background. *(Crown Copyright, 2012 LA(Phot) Keith Morgan)*

Facility that provides specialised first aid, triage, resuscitation, stabilisation and preparation of serious casualties for evacuation to higher-level facilities. Prior to hostilities it is possible to embark a surgical team and equipment to enhance the capability to Role 2. This provides a wider range of medical and nursing interventions and enhanced medical facilities.

The ship's sickbay suite comprises a surgery and a ward that can be a separate quarantine area. The sickbay is three times the size of those on earlier frigates and destroyers and is used during normal duties to provide primary health care to the ship's complement, medical advice to the command and the treatment of sick and injured personnel. The on-board medical team constantly test and enhance the sailors' and marines' life-saving skills in preparation for every eventuality.

Anti-surface warfare (ASuW)

Type 45 destroyers are not, as yet, fitted with anti-ship missiles. In order to meet their ASuW role of assisting the naval group in establishing control of the sea area of operations the destroyers are fitted with guns and have an embarked helicopter that can engage surface targets.

The Lynx helicopter can range a long way

ABOVE Ward area of HMS *Defender*'s sickbay. *(Crown Copyright, 2012 HMS Defender)*

LEFT Marine practising the insertion of intravenous drips under the supervision of HMS *Diamond*'s surgeon. *(Crown Copyright, 2012 LA(Phot) Gary Weatherston)*

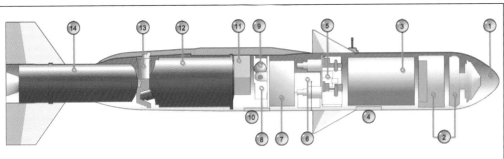

1 Radome.	5 Control surface motors.	10 Altimeter transmitter antenna.
2 Homing head.	6 Thermal batteries.	11 Altimeter data processing unit.
3 Warhead and safety and arming unit.	7 Electronics pack.	12 Sustainer motor.
4 Altimeter receiver antenna.	8 Gyros.	13 Motor ignition delay unit.
	9 Gas bottle.	14 Boost motor.

LEFT Cutaway of a Sea Skua missile. *(Author/MBDA UK illustration)*

127

its final approach. Its impact-delayed fuze postpones detonation of the 28kg blast-fragmentation warhead until Sea Skua has penetrated the target's hull.

The Lynx's radar is capable of operating in a 'track while scan' mode, illuminating the missile's target with a radar beam while scanning for other targets. The helicopter's heading must remain within 80° of the missile trajectory to maintain illumination.

Anti-submarine warfare (ASW)

The Type 2091 bow-mounted sonar is capable of detecting, tracking and classifying submarines. It can also warn of mines and torpedoes. The sonar is not as sensitive as the towed-array sonars deployed by the Type 23 frigates, whose primary role is ASW; however, Type 45 destroyers can provide support to ASW operations. The Lynx helicopter can carry dipping sonars to locate submarines and Sting Ray torpedoes to prosecute enemy submarines. The Sting Ray Mod 1 is a lightweight, air-launched, electrically powered homing torpedo for use against all submarine targets. It combines low noise and excellent manoeuvrability with a high-speed attack capability. Sting Ray is an autonomous weapon. Before launch it receives information from the helicopter that dictates the search pattern that its active sonar and tactical software will use to pinpoint its submarine target. The torpedo's software enables it to destroy submarines with its highly lethal warhead even if the submarine deploys complex countermeasures.

from the ship and attack hostile vessels beyond the ship's horizon both in the open ocean and the littoral. For this purpose it carries Sea Skua missiles with a range of 25km. The Lynx searches for its target using its Seaspray radar. Once a target is located, Seaspray illuminates the target and the Sea Skua's semi-active homing-head detects the reflected energy. The missile is then dropped from its retaining rack and, once free of the Lynx, its motor fires.

As the missile drops, its trajectory levels out just above the sea's surface. If the sea is calm the missile can fly close to the surface to avoid detection, but in rough seas it needs to fly higher. Before launch Sea Skua is programmed to travel at one of four pre-selected heights. After 75 to 125sec, close to the target, the missile climbs to a height at which the missile's radar can again detect the Lynx's reflected radar beam and so reacquire the target for

After being launched from a Lynx or Merlin helicopter, the torpedo's descent is slowed by a parachute that ensures it is travelling at the correct speed and angle for entering the water. The main power source for Sting Ray is a magnesium/silver chloride battery with a seawater electrolyte that activates once the torpedo is submerged. The torpedo then starts its propulsion system and discards its parachute.

On entering the water, the Sting Ray torpedo carries out an immediate check to determine water depth. If it is shallow, the torpedo runs at a fixed height following the contours of

BELOW **Sting Ray Mk3 lightweight torpedo dropped from a Lynx helicopter.** *(Crown Copyright, 2008)*

the seabed; in deeper water it searches a vertical column of water where the submarine has previously been detected. The torpedo's on-board computer, which controls the acoustics and the homing and attack profile, carries out a search pattern based upon the pre-launch inputs of safety ceiling, initial search depth, magnetic variation and torpedo heading, until the target has been located. The target is classified and identified from the return signals and, once acquired, the torpedo starts homing on to it. The torpedo is able to determine the target's speed, heading and depth, thus enabling the weapon to select the best attack profile, as well as the optimum aim-point and impact angle.

The insensitive munition warhead generates a significant isotropic blast effect, and its shaped charge produces a highly directional jet of molten metal to penetrate the pressure hull of the submarine and inflict catastrophic damage. By accurately placing the warhead at near normal incidence to the submarine, the torpedo's guidance system ensures a high lethality by affording the maximum potential to penetrate a submarine pressure hull.

Should the Sting Ray miss its target, it has the ability to turn and engage in a second attack.

Despite Lynx's ASW capabilities, Merlin helicopters remain the RN's main platform for submarine search and prosecution because of their sensitive dipping sonar and ability to deploy sonobuoys. However, Type 45 destroyers are able to refuel these helicopters and rearm them with their Sting Ray torpedoes.

LEFT Sequence of Merlin helicopter dropping a Sting Ray torpedo. *(Crown Copyright, 1999)*

Maritime security operations

A major peacetime role of Type 45 destroyers is to undertake maritime security operations to prevent piracy, terrorism, smuggling, drug-running, people-trafficking and other crimes. Undertaken in coordination with other nations' military units, these missions are to interdict shipping, enforce embargoes and support civil authorities worldwide. Type 45 destroyers are able to stop and search a wide range of vessels and to board vessels whether they comply or resist requests to search them. RN warships are able to detain small numbers of suspects for short periods pending delivery to an appropriate law enforcement agency.

Pirates use small vessels (known as skiffs), and those of smugglers and drug-runners are usually also very fast. The 30mm SCGs and the

JACKSPEAK

A fast boat used by criminals, especially in the Caribbean, is described as a 'go-fast'.

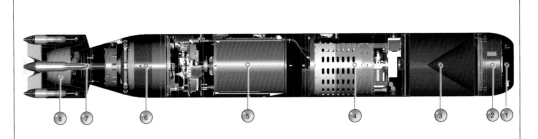

1 Sonar transducer array.
2 Digital active/passive sonar homing system.
3 Shaped charge insensitive munition warhead.
4 Control electronics.

5 Magnesium/silver chloride seawater battery.
6 Contra-rotating electric motor.
7 High-rate electro-mechanical actuation system.
8 Ducted pump jet propulsor.

LEFT Cutaway of a Sting Ray torpedo. *(Author/BAE Systems illustration)*

Miniguns, designed to prevent attack by fast inshore attack craft, can literally put a warning shot across their bows. Usually the warning is heeded and an armed boarding party, using the ship's RIBs, will board suspect vessels and search them.

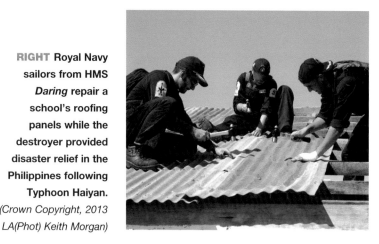

Humanitarian aid and disaster relief (HADR) operations

Warships, especially those as capable as Type 45 destroyers, with their highly trained and versatile personnel, are ideally suited to assist in emergencies. Their tasks include the protection of UK citizens (and, if necessary non-combatant evacuation operations), humanitarian operations, disaster relief and defence diplomacy. The destroyers – with their own power, water supplies, medical facilities and communications – will be able to contribute to emergencies even with little or no local support, as they can operate without access to commercial ports or airfields.

Type 45 destroyers have the administrative infrastructure to act as an evacuation handling centre and provide basic accommodation, sustenance and medical services. They have emergency accommodation for at least 200 evacuees and, if necessary, 700 evacuees for up to two days.

All military organisations can turn their skills to a number of other tasks to assist Civil Powers at home or abroad; for example, search and rescue operations or HADR operations. In time of crisis, the destroyers are able to give a first response. Not only can they provide basic security, assured communications, food, drinking water and medical assistance, but also the manpower to deliver basic repair to life-support services. Dependent upon the prevailing conditions, many of the ship's company may be able to respond. For instance, if the ship is at anchor over half the personnel may be able to assist ashore without compromising the ship's safety. A classic example of cross-government HADR occurred in late 2013 in the disaster relief effort following Typhoon Haiyan. HMS *Daring* was exercising in the Far East when she was diverted to assist the Philippines in conjunction with RAF C17 and C130 aircraft and HMS *Illustrious*. HMS *Daring* was first on the scene for the UK and liaised with the Department for International Development representative and the British Embassy, along with other non-government organisations. She was able to deliver food, water, first aid and temporary shelter to several remote communities only accessible by sea. The destroyer was a source of fresh water, medical assistance and much-needed technical expertise. Ongoing assistance to re-establish the communities' infrastructure included the installation of desalination plants in wells contaminated with seawater as well as the repair of key facilities such as buildings and the damaged engines of fishing boats.

Storing, replenishment at sea and VERTREP

Before departing on operations warships are loaded with victuals, ammunition and consumable general naval stores. For Type 45 destroyers this is usually carried out by dockside cranes lifting stores to 01-Deck, where they are taken to the stores lift and struck down into storage. An alternative route is to lift stores on to the flight deck (using dockside cranes or the boat bay's davit) and through the hangar to the lift. Fuel is also taken on and, immediately before the destroyers leave their Portsmouth home base, missiles are loaded at the new purpose-built Upper Harbour Ammunitioning Facility.

Although Type 45 destroyers have a long range, once on deployment it is a seamanlike precaution to take on fuel and stores whenever possible. At sea the transfer of fuel and stores from RFA ships (and those of other nations contributing to operations) is achieved by an evolution called

JACKSPEAK

The home port for Type 45 destroyers is Portsmouth – affectionately known as Pompey.

ABOVE HMS *Daring* loading stores dockside in Her Majesty's Naval Base, Portsmouth, before her planned maiden operational deployment east of Suez. *(Crown Copyright, 2012 LA(Phot) Keith Morgan)*

'replenishment at sea'. To allow replenishment on to 01-Deck from ships to port or starboard (or even both, simultaneously) the destroyers are fitted with four moveable high-points. Each of these consists of a vertically moving trolley, housed within a fabricated framework running on four hardened steel rollers, and a swivel bracket and eyeplates. The moveable high-points are two-decks high and normally hidden behind a door. The trolley allows a heavy jackstay to be hauled up to 03-Deck level.

Replenishment at sea is perhaps the single most dangerous evolution carried out by the

BELOW Artist's impression of a Type 45 destroyer undergoing fuel replenishment at sea and helicopter vertical replenishment from the Military Afloat Reach and Sustainability (MARS) tanker RFA *Tidespring* (due to enter service in 2016). *(BMT Group)*

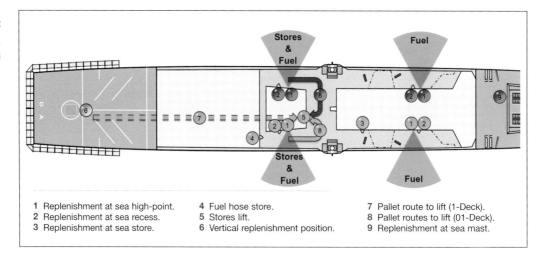

RIGHT Replenishment
at sea facilities.
(Author)

1 Replenishment at sea high-point.
2 Replenishment at sea recess.
3 Replenishment at sea store.
4 Fuel hose store.
5 Stores lift.
6 Vertical replenishment position.
7 Pallet route to lift (1-Deck).
8 Pallet routes to lift (01-Deck).
9 Replenishment at sea mast.

RN in peacetime. The seamanship challenge is for the warship and the supply ship (which may be over twice the size of a destroyer) to sail on parallel courses a mere 40m apart. They must adopt exactly the same speed and travel in excess of 10 knots (20km/h) while they are linked together by the heavy tensioned cables used to transfer supplies and support fuel pipes. It is vital that transfers are carried out safely and completed quickly.

To transfer fuel, the destroyer's team fire a gunline to the supply ship. The supply ship attaches the heavy jackstay wire so it can be hauled across to the warship. Once the jackstay wire is attached to the destroyer, an auto-tensioning winch on the supply ship brings it

RIGHT HMS
Diamond **performing
replenishment at
sea of fuel to both
port and starboard
forward positions:
(a) firing gunline;
(b) hauling in heavy
jackstay wire with
gunline; (c) fuel hose
travelling towards
destroyer on three
runner winches; and
(d) hose connected
to fuelling point.**
*(Crown Copyright,
2010 LA(Phot) Gary
Weatherston)*

under tension. The jackstay wire will normally sit at a slight downward angle from the supply ship, so the fuel hose can be lowered down the jackstay to the receiving ship using runner winches. The probe at the end of the hose mates with a probe reception point on the warship. Once the hose is connected refuelling can begin. Fuel flows from the supply ship to the reception point and through temporary hoses and fixed pipework into the fuel tanks.

The transfer of supplies also requires a heavy jackstay, but once it is connected to the destroyer's moveable high-point it is hoisted so that the loads slung beneath it can be deposited on 01-Deck. Loads are usually supplied on pallets, and two-tonne loads are attached to a traveller block that can be moved along the jackstay by outhauls. A light jackstay wire is used for the transfer of personnel (in both directions) using a boson's chair slung from the traveller block.

As the destroyer receives supply pallets, they are lowered on to trollies that transfer them the short distance on 01-Deck to the stores lift. From there they descend to pallet stores. On the earlier Type 42 destroyers supplies had to be broken down into lighter loads and passed by human chains down to the stores – an operation that required most of the ship's personnel. To store a destroyer for 90 days requires large quantities of consumables and victuals, including 150 loaves of bread, 200 litres of soup, 50kg bacon, 2,000 tea bags, 1,500 eggs and a tonne of potatoes. With the pallet and lift system, ten sailors can load 90 days of stores in a single day. In future it is intended to introduce a heavy replenishment at sea system that can transfer loads of five tonnes, with a further increase of efficiency.

Between the forward superstructure and Sea Viper silo on 1-Deck is a mast that can also be raised for light jackstay transfers of personnel or light stores.

The ship's helicopter can also be used to transfer stores – an operation termed VERTREP (vertical replenishment). The loads are limited by the carrying capacity of the helicopter. However, the supplying ship does not need to be in close proximity or even have a flight deck, as the supplies can be attached to the helicopter when hovering. VERTREP is useful to collect materiel such as additional medical supplies.

ABOVE HMS *Dragon* trial light jackstay transfer of a mannequin by boson's chair from RFA *Orangeleaf*. *(Crown Copyright, 2012)*

LEFT HMS *Dragon*'s Lynx helicopter performing VERTREP. *(Crown Copyright, 2013 LA(Phot) Dave Jenkins)*

BELOW Aft side of coaming, Sea Viper silo bay, with stowed replenishment at sea mast. *(Daniel Ferro)*

Chapter Five

The future

Warfare is continually evolving with potential threats becoming increasingly difficult to detect and to defeat. The destroyers have been designed at modest cost so that their capability can be readily enhanced during their life. They can accommodate improved equipment already in development and future advances as they become available.

OPPOSITE Artist's impression of a Type 45 destroyer with a 'Queen Elizabeth' class aircraft carrier. The carrier is due to achieve operational military capability in 2020. *(BAE Systems)*

Incremental Acquisition Programme (IAP)

A well-designed and well-maintained warship can remain in service for 30 years or more. However, as threats evolve, and as the elements of the combat system are developed to meet these threats, it is essential that ships are flexible enough to allow modification. Consequently, Type 45 destroyers have been designed to maintain their versatility to meet the unpredictably changing roles that they may be called upon to perform. Not only does the hull have margins of weight, space and stability, but the ship's services (power, ventilation and cooling) also have spare capacity for future enhancements. Several of the ships' compartments have been purposely unallocated, or contain spare space to allow the installation of additional equipment. The flight deck of Type 45 destroyers is four times the area of that of Type 42 destroyers (which also operated Lynx helicopters). They are equipped as well with the most modern aviation facilities, so can operate not only the Lynx and Merlin helicopters and their successors but are also big enough to land a Chinook twin-rotor helicopter.

During the design period potential combat systems equipment was assessed for cost-effectiveness in meeting the destroyers' primary roles. The installation of some elements was deferred to save time and cost. 'Installation provision made in design' is the term used to ensure that it is possible to fit specific additional combat system capability at a later date. Generally the ships were not designed as fitted to receive existing equipment, as this would have meant including cabling or pipework so that the equipment could be installed immediately with no further changes to the ship. A decade after the destroyers were designed it was clear that there were already increasing threats from theatre ballistic missiles and from hard to detect targets like unmanned airborne vehicles.

IAP intends to upgrade capability through the life of the warship by adding new or improved equipment. This equipment includes those whose fitting was deferred and items under development or due to enter service after the ships' operational dates. Potential enhancements identified during design were:

- Phalanx 1B close-in weapon system.
- Tomahawk land attack missiles or 155mm Naval Gun (under development).
- Cooperative engagement capability.
- Surface ship guided weapons system.
- Surface ship torpedo defence.
- Twin-tubed fixed magazine torpedo launch system (port and starboard).
- Communications electronic support measures.

In fact, the Phalanx system entered RN service in 2007 and was fitted to the Type 45 destroyers before they were accepted into service.

The software open architecture adopted by CMS-1 will also allow equipment's software to be upgraded in order to enhance the combat capability. The Maritime Integration and Support Centre used to develop and test the combat system will continue to be used to improve and validate the destroyers' combat system software. The Centre remains important not only for software development but for integrating IAP equipment into the combat system.

Tomahawk land attack missiles (TLAM)

The destroyers' design incorporated specific growth margins for two modular eight-cell Mk41 strike-length vertical launch silos. These can accommodate TLAM to provide a long-range strike capability. The space located between the MCG and Sea Viper silos is sufficient for these launchers, which are considerably deeper than the Sylver A-50 launchers. The TLAM cruise missiles, with a range of 1,300km, are

BELOW Tomahawk land attack missile. *(Crown Copyright, 2000)*

the weapon of choice for long-range precision attacks. An anti-ship version has been developed and, if included in the missile mix of the launcher would give the force a capability that could not be provided by frigates.

Since the completion of the Type 45 destroyer's design definition in 2003, a *missile de croisière naval* (naval cruise missile) has been developed for the French Navy. A naval variant of the air-launched Storm Shadow, this missile fits the Sylver A-70 launchers, two of which could be fitted instead of the two Mk41 launchers.

Eight-cell vertical launchers			
	Footprint	Height	Weight (empty)
Sylver A-50 (current)	4.2m x 3.1m*	6.0m	8,000kg
Sylver A-70	4.2m x 3.1m*	7.6m	12,000kg
Strike-length Mk41	3.2m x 2.1m	7.7m	14,500kg
* Sylver dimensions include an operational envelope of 0.8m on both sides and one end.			

Theatre ballistic missile defence (TBMD)

Over 30 countries, including some 'rogue states', have acquired or are in the process of acquiring theatre ballistic missile (TBM) technology. Ballistic missiles can be used to carry not only conventional warheads, but also weapons of mass destruction. They threaten naval forces or amphibious landings and may overfly a force to target friendly territory. TBMs include both short-range ballistic missiles whose range is up to 1,000km and medium-range

ballistic missiles with ranges between 1,000km and 3,000km. Type 45 destroyers were not originally required to combat such missiles, but TBMs now pose an increasing danger. The destroyers could be adapted to counter them if fitted with missiles currently under development in NATO countries.

There is not currently an urgent need to deploy TBMD but, given the long gestation of such systems, some work has been undertaken preparing for a possible requirement. In December 2011 a French trial was performed in which a current Aster-30 (now termed Aster-30 Block I) successfully intercepted a Black Sparrow target missile. This target missile flew in a manner that represented the trajectory of a short-range ballistic missile. The Aster-30 was launched from a land-based Sylver launcher and the target was detected and tracked by a French Army version of the Arabel radar (rather than the Empar radar fitted to their two frigates). The Sampson MFR could potentially give more warning of ballistic threats and better detection of the missiles. Work started in 2012 to investigate improvements to Sampson MFR to detect and track ballistic missiles and satellites in high orbit.

Black Sparrow ballistic missile target	
Threat representation	SCUD-B
Pre-launch weight	1,275kg
Length	4.85m
Diameter	526mm
Navigation system	Inertial/GPS
Flight termination system	Dual redundant
Telemetry system	Two channels, omnidirectional coverage
Warhead simulation section	Common, modular, mission selectable
Electronics section	Common, test range adaptable
Motor	Solid propellant rocket motor

Incremental improvements to Aster-30 (called Aster Block I New Technology) were also started in 2011. The new missile will have the same dimensions as the existing Aster-30 but will have a new booster, giving it a substantially increased range. However, some concerns

FAR LEFT Mk41 strike-length vertical launch system. *(BAE Systems)*

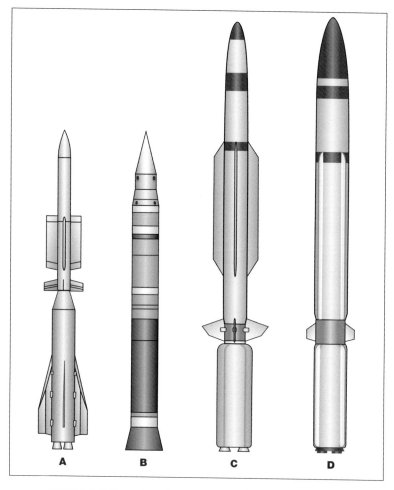

thrust-to-weight ratio than the Block I missiles. The first propulsion stage of Aster Block II will accelerate it to close to Mach 6. The second propulsion stage will increase this to above Mach 7. This stage will allow continuous control of the interceptor until Aster's warhead (Kill Vehicle) is released several seconds before interception. The Kill Vehicle has an imaging infrared seeker to track the ballistic missile.

The challenge of destroying an incoming ballistic missile has been likened to 'hitting a bullet with a bullet'. To provide the exceptional accuracy and agility needed as it is guided towards its target, the Kill Vehicle will have a divert and attitude control system. This system will have two means of controlling the final trajectory of the Kill Vehicle. Four compact divert valves use powerful electro-mechanical actuators to provide a very high thrust very quickly in order to adjust the speed of the Kill Vehicle. Six attitude control system external valves are linked to the gas generator chamber and use fast-acting electro-mechanical actuators to alter the attitude of the Kill Vehicle as it approaches its target.

Aster Block II is unlikely to be available before 2020.

Apart from the European Aster family of missile systems there are also US systems that could provide TBMD. They are all fired from the strike-length Mk41 vertical launch system that could be installed on Type 45 destroyers. The proposed US missile capable of use against medium-range ballistic missiles is the standard missile SM-3 Block IB (RIM-161C).

The SM-3 Block IB is a development of the SM-3 Block IA (RIM-161B) missile. While Block IA used a single-frequency infrared seeker, Block IB employs an enhanced dual-frequency infrared seeker with data fusion. In addition, it has a throttleable divert and attitude control system that employs short bursts of precision propulsion to steer the missile toward incoming targets.

In mid-2012 USS *Lake Erie* (CG70) launched a SM-3 Block IB interceptor during a test. The SM-3 missile successfully intercepted a separating ballistic missile target. The ship had detected and tracked the target, and its weapons system developed a fire control solution. The target was intercepted a few minutes after launch

have been expressed that the gain in range has been achieved by a reduction of speed that would reduce Aster-30's primary, medium-range defensive role. The new Aster will have a dual-role warhead that could be configured before launch to destroy either conventional or ballistic missiles. A new radar seeker with a higher waveform has also been proposed for the missile, in order to more accurately determine the optimum point of impact.

Also begun in 2011 was a Technology Demonstrator Programme for Aster Block II, a missile dedicated to countering highly manoeuvrable TBMs whose warheads separate to release decoy warheads. Aimed to fit in the same A-50 Sylver launcher as Aster Block I, the new missile will have no wings and can therefore have a larger diameter body (450mm). It is intended to intercept ballistic missiles with ranges of over 3,000km before they re-enter the atmosphere. Aster Block II will target the missile or the warhead if this has already separated from the missile body. It will have a higher

with about the same kinetic energy as a 10-tonne truck travelling at 1,000km/h.

A further phase of development, the SM-3 Block IIA, is planned against intermediate-range ballistic missiles (3,000 to 5,000km range). This would have an advanced warhead with a high-divert attitude control system to improve target acquisition and a 512 x 512 focal-plane array seeker with advanced signal processing to enhance discrimination. To achieve the range, the missile body would be larger but it would remain compatible with the standard missile canisters and the Mk41 vertical launch system.

SM-3 Block IB is due for delivery to US forces in 2015, with the SM-3 Block IIA planned for 2018.

Like TLAM, SM-3 missiles are fired from the Mk41 strike-length launcher. These launchers are well established worldwide, with ten times more missile cells in service than Sylver launchers, and are in service with no fewer than 11 navies. The Type 45 destroyer's design includes a void beneath the current Sylver A-50 launchers that would allow six Mk41 strike-length launchers to be substituted. Currently the Mk41 launchers are not qualified to launch Aster missiles, but if such qualification trials were undertaken then the destroyers could have 64 cells loaded with a mix of Aster-15, Aster-30, TLAM and SM-3 missiles.

LEFT **Standard missile SM-3 Block IB launched by USS** Lake Erie **against a ballistic missile target during trials.** (USN Photo, 2012)

155mm Naval Gun (Third-Generation Maritime Fire)

An alternative upgrade that would occupy the space allocated to two Mk41 launchers would be the 155mm Naval Gun. This would replace the 114mm MCG. However, fitting the 155mm Naval Gun would preclude the future fitting of Tomahawk variants or US missiles to counter TBMs. The gun would see the 6m barrel from the Army's AS90 Braveheart self-propelled howitzer grafted on to the robust existing Mk8 naval mounting. This mounting would provide, among other things, stabilisation against ship motion. Only minor changes would be required, affecting only 20% of the mounting. A 155mm gun would not only provide an increased projectile size but also a small increase in range from 24 to 30km.

BELOW **AS90 Braveheart 155mm self-propelled howitzer.** (Crown Copyright, 2003 Corporal Paul (Jabba) Jarv)

Missiles for longer vertical launchers			
	Standard SM-3 Block I	MdCN	TLAM
Role	TBMD	Land attack	Land attack*
Pre-launch weight	1,500kg	1,500kg	1,600kg
Length	6.55m	5.1m	6.25m
Range	>500km	>1,000km	1,700km
Speed	9,600km/h	1,000km/h	
Navigation system	GPS/ inertial and semi-active radar	Tercom/ GPS/ inertial	Tercom/ GPS/ inertial
Homing	Imaging IR	Imaging IR	DSMAC
Warhead	LEAP	50kg BROACH	450kg Bullpup
* Anti-ship version also available with similar physical characteristics.			

A potential increase of the barrel length to 8m would significantly increase the range to up to 40km. The muzzle energy of the new gun is double that of the existing MCG, necessitating additional steel strengthening to the interface of the deck and the mounting. This increase in weight and modifications to the mount (which adds a further 2,000kg) has been allowed for in the ship's design margins.

The 155mm gun offers commonality with land artillery systems by only adopting a system using modular propellant charges that are loaded separately from the shell in the turret. Naval guns moved away from this approach, based on bag charges, several decades ago. The use of naval systems using rigid cases instead or integrated shells could require redesign of the gun itself. The rates of fire of larger guns is slower than smaller guns, so the total weight of projectiles delivered in a given period may be lower, albeit mitigated by the psychological impact of each large projectile. Solutions to the problems include automatic loading and water-cooling. However, these add further weight.

While the 155mm gun may be accommodated on the destroyers, the gun and its associated strengthening may be too heavy for frigates, so the penalty of adopting it may be a loss of ammunition commonality across the fleet.

Autonomous small-calibre guns (ASCG)

The RN is replacing its DSB30B on Type 23 frigates with a modified version of the SCG mounting, featuring remote control via a video link and the replacement of the Oerlikon KCB with an ATK Mk44 cannon. The frigate's system is linked to an earlier EOGCS. The new ASCG system is designated Seahawk DS30M Mk2. The change to a more advanced cannon results in a significant fall in the rate of fire (from 600 to 200 rounds/min). However, this is considered acceptable, as the primary targets are no longer aircraft, for which a high rate of fire is essential, but small boats. It is anticipated that Type 45 destroyers will be fitted at some point with the new cannons linked to its more advanced EOGCS.

Harpoon surface ship guided weapon (SSGW) system (Guided Weapon System 60)

Provision has been made to fit a SSGW system based on the GWS 60 Harpoon Block IC over-the-horizon anti-ship missile that is currently fitted to Type 23 frigates. Fixed canister quad-launchers would be mounted athwartships port and starboard between the superstructure and the Sea Viper silos. Although first introduced into service with the USN in 1977, the Harpoon missile has undergone a series of incremental upgrades and is considered a very effective anti-ship weapon. It is in service in over 600 ships worldwide. There are also submarine- and aircraft-launched versions.

The Harpoon Block II (RGM-84L) system could be installed instead of the Block IC. This missile entered service with the Royal Danish Navy in 2001 and incorporates a new guidance control unit that provides greater accuracy against surface ships and can distinguish between ships and islands. This gives the missile an anti-ship capability in coastal regions as well as a capability against land targets.

Harpoon surface ship guided weapons system missiles		
	Harpoon Block IC	Harpoon Block II
Role	Anti-surface ship	Anti-surface ship and land attack
Trajectory	Sea-skimming	Sea-skimming
Pre-launch weight	681kg	681kg
Length	4.6m	4.6m
Diameter	340mm	340mm
Range	120km	120km
Speed	>860km/h	>860km/h
Propulsion	Solid boost/turbojet	Solid boost/turbojet
Navigation system	Inertial	Inertial measurement unit/GPS
Homing	On-board J-band radar	On-board J-band radar
Warhead	227kg	227kg

ASW frigates are more likely to require anti-ship capability than AAW destroyers, as frigates searching for submarines tend to operate towards the edge of a task force. Nevertheless, a SSGW system would be a useful capability for Type 45 destroyers, as they will not always be operating from the centre of a task group. The land attack capability would be an adjunct to their ability to assist in amphibious operations.

Surface ship torpedo defence (SSTD) Type 2170

The threat of torpedo attack has proliferated with the increase of the number of quiet, conventionally powered submarines. ASW frigates are already fitted with SSTD to protect them from this threat, and provision to fit the system has been made in the design of the Type 45 destroyers. Destroyers are protected against submarine attack by the frigates; however, there is always the possibility of a hostile submarine penetrating these defences. The attractiveness of the destroyers as a target would make torpedo defence a valuable Type 45 destroyer capability.

SSTD's sensor is a multi-octave, acoustic, towed-array sonar comprising a row of hydrophones towed behind the ship. A dedicated single-drum winch deploys and recovers the array. A fibre-optic signal cable carried by the tow cable connects the array's detectors to the ship. This sonar uses noise emitted by incoming torpedoes to detect, classify and accurately locate them. The system advises on the best course for the ship to steer and the timing of activation of not only towed decoys but also the deployment of expendable acoustic devices to act as decoys. The latter are fired from eight-barrelled mortar launchers that use high pressure air from a self-contained reservoir to propel them into the water close to the warship. The flight time is very fast, and the device can emit a decoy acoustic signal within ten seconds of entering the water.

The trend is for torpedoes to become quieter and so harder to detect passively at

tactically significant ranges. As a consequence, the equipment manufacturer is developing a new generation of SSTD that will use active detection, classification and location. The active system will use a towed, active, in-line source to emit acoustic pulses and detect reflections from incoming torpedoes. The system will have the ability to detect salvoes of torpedoes and

ABOVE Type 23 Frigate, HMS *Montrose*, firing a Harpoon anti-ship missile. *(Crown Copyright, 2013 PO(Phot) Wheelie A'barrow)*

RIGHT An expendable acoustic device being loaded into the Type 2071 surface ship torpedo defence system launcher. *(Ultra Electronics)*

will have the advantage over passive detection of being less dependent on the vagaries associated with ever-changing water conditions. A pre-production model is expected in 2014.

Surface ship torpedo defence system Type 2170			
	Winch	Launcher	Expendable acoustic device
Height	1.7m	1.7m	420mm
Width	1.9m	1.2m	120mm
Depth	2.2m	1.6m	diameter
Weight	4,200kg	583kg	7.5kg

Communications electronic support measures (CESM)

A CESM system monitors communications signals in order to determine the purpose of potential adversaries from their intercepted transmissions. The intention is to fit a new maritime CESM system to Type 45 destroyers under Project Shaman. The MoD has agreed to purchase the US AN/SSQ-137(V) ship signal exploitation equipment increment F. This equipment, the major component of the CESM system, acquires, identifies, locates and analyses communications signals by using the latest in field-programmable, gate-array, embedded processors and advanced server network technologies. This off-the-shelf solution

is part of a wider programme architecture known as Seaseeker. The new communications eavesdropping system, known as Seaseeker-Shaman, also includes selective availability anti-spoofing modules, GPS receivers and system signal and direction-finding stimulator packages.

To improve the UK's shipborne signals intelligence and surveillance capability seven systems will be fitted to selected Type 45 destroyers, and will also replace the cooperative outboard logistics update communications electronic support measures suite on Type 23 frigates.

Data-links

Current RN warships are fitted with two data-link systems, Link-11 and Link-16, which enable them to exchange tactical digital information with other ships, aircraft and land forces. Link-11 dates to the 1950s and is a secure half-duplex link that transmits data at 1.8kb/sec at HF and 12.7kb/sec at UHF. At high latitudes or in poor transmission conditions it may not be possible to establish a link. The system relies on one platform to control the network and to report positional information on sensor detections. As a consequence, it lacks robustness in the event that the controlling ship is lost or suffers an equipment failure.

Link-16 is a secure, jam-resistant 54kb/sec digital data-link that allows voice communication but is limited to line-of-sight transmissions.

Type 45 destroyers could be fitted with a new data-link, Link-22, under the NATO Improved Link-11 programme. Link-22 provides a beyond line-of-sight, secure, tactical digital communications capability, supporting the exchange of information. All friendly air, surface, sub-surface and land platforms can thus generate an enhanced tactical picture based on common data. Link-22 transmits data at up to 4.1Mb/sec at HF and 12.7Mb/sec at UHF. Unlike Link-11, it can simultaneously transmit different signals on as many as four networks to increase the bandwidth.

Link-22 will feature:

- Highly secure communications protocols.
- Multiple networks.
- Automatic relay of digital messages.

BELOW Schematic of data-link systems. *(Author from Northrop Grumman information)*

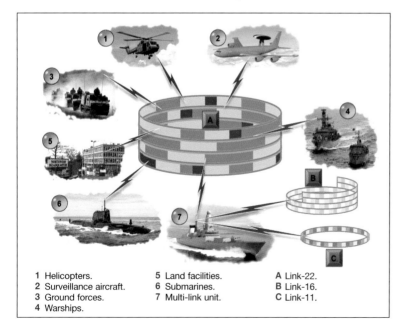

1 Helicopters.
2 Surveillance aircraft.
3 Ground forces.
4 Warships.
5 Land facilities.
6 Submarines.
7 Multi-link unit.
A Link-22.
B Link-16.
C Link-11.

- Reliable beyond line-of-sight communications.
- Distributed protocols that ensure a robust network in the event of loss of ships.
- Automatic congestion management.

The addition of Link-22 will greatly improve NATO interoperability and, by providing better situational awareness, will enhance the war-fighting capability of the Type 45 destroyer's command team.

Cooperative engagement capability (CEC)

Currently warships build a picture of the threat environment from information provided by their own sensors, supplemented by data from other ships and aircraft passed over digital data-links. The complex representation of the surface and air tracks of friendly and hostile entities is generated from the perspective of the ship. The warfare that it conducts is described as platform-centric.

The USN is proposing a fundamental shift towards network-centric warfare, in which friendly forces establish information superiority by networking all sensors of the force to achieve a single, shared, force-wide situational awareness. By enabling many ships, aircraft and land forces to pool their radar and sensor information, their combined resources create a very accurate and detailed picture that is much finer, more wide ranging, and more consistent than any one of these units could generate on its own. Information superiority inevitably translates into greater combat effectiveness. To achieve the maximum benefits of this approach, it is necessary for the US's major NATO partners to have ships and aircraft equipped for such warfare.

Radar electronic support measures (RESM) Outfit UAT Mod 2.0

Since entering operational service HMS *Daring*'s and HMS *Diamond*'s RESM has been updated to Outfit UAT Mod 2.0. A further development, Mod 2.1, will be rolled out to the whole class. The changes include direct radio frequency sampling, better emitter identification technology and new digital antennas. The equipment will provide improved system performance in the modern, dense radar environment, enabling the ship to operate more effectively in all operational maritime theatres, including the littoral environment.

By digitising the signals at the antenna, the majority of the receiver's functionality is now implemented using software and firmware algorithms. This will make it easier to introduce further incremental enhancements and to implement new signal analysis tools. RESM capability can then quickly adapt to the rapidly evolving operational environment.

The approach adopted for the programme maximises the use of commercial off-the-shelf hardware, making the equipment significantly more reliable and easier to maintain so lowering the total cost of ownership.

Lynx Wildcat Mk1 HMA (Helicopter Maritime Attack)

The Lynx Wildcat Mk1 naval variant (HMA2) will replace the current Lynx helicopter when it is declared operational in 2015. It has a redesigned tail that accommodates a more powerful tail rotor system as well as improved strength and stealth qualities. In addition to

BELOW Lynx Wildcat Mk1 HMA (Helicopter Maritime Attack).
(AgustaWestland)

Comparison of the Lynx and Lynx Wildcat helicopters

	Lynx Mk8 SUR	Lynx Wildcat
Top speed	334km/h	290km/h
Crew	Pilot and observer	Pilot and observer
Height	3.7m	3.73m
Length	13.4m	15.22m
Range	600km	780km
Engine power	2 x 750kW	2 x 1,016kW
Main rotor	12.8m diameter	12.8m diameter
Unladen weight	3,291kg	4,700kg
Max all-up mass	5,330kg	6,000kg
Sensors		
Radar	Seaspray 3000	Seaspray 7000E
Infrared	SeaOwl	Wescam MX-15Di electro-optical/laser designator
Armament		
Door-mount		M3M 0.5in heavy machine gun
Missiles	4 Sea Skua	4 *Anti-Navire Léger* missiles or 14 Lightweight Multi-Role Missiles
or torpedoes	2 Sting Ray MOD1	2 Sting Ray MOD1
or depth charges	2	2

Comparison of Sea Skua missile and its replacements

	Sea Skua missile	*Anti-Navire Léger* missile	Lightweight Multi-Role Missile
Weight	145kg	≈110kg	13kg
No carried	4	4	14
Length	2.5m	≈2.5m	1.3m
Diameter	0.25m	≈0.2m	0.076m
Wingspan	0.72m		
Warhead	30kg semi-armour-piercing, 9kg RDX	40kg blast-fragmentation	3kg blast
Detonation	delayed detonation impact fuze		Laser proximity sensor
Propulsion	solid fuel booster/ solid fuel sustain	solid fuel booster/ solid fuel sustain	two-stage solid propellant
Range	25km		6 to 8km
Speed	>980km/h	≈1,000km/h	≈1,800km/h
Guidance	Semi-active radar	Infrared seeker autonomous or operator guided	Laser beam-riding and/ or semi-active laser with infrared terminal homing

these visual differences, the Wildcat has two 1,015kW LHTEC CTS800-4N engines that provide 37% more power than the current Lynx engines. This will give improved performance, especially when operating in hot environments (48°C) and at high altitudes. The cockpit instrumentation, communications, 360° full-colour surveillance radar and electro-optical/laser designator targeting systems all provide substantial performance improvements over existing systems. Its radar, the 110kg Seaspray 7000E active electronically scanned array, forms a pencil beam that is positioned electronically vertically, but in azimuth combines mechanical and electronic scanning.

To engage ships of up to 1,000 tonnes the Wildcat will be armed with the *Anti-Navire Léger* missile once this enters service. The missile offers high (but subsonic) speed, stand-off operation, minimum sensor-to-effect time and autonomous guidance from a new, uncooled infrared seeker. However, a data-link will relay the target image back to the helicopter so the operator can change the profile of the missile's flight right up to the point of impact. This will offer a high level of target discrimination, some degree of aim-point selection and, if necessary, mission abort. The missile is initially propelled

BELOW Artist's impression of *Anti-Navire Léger* missile. *(MBDA)*

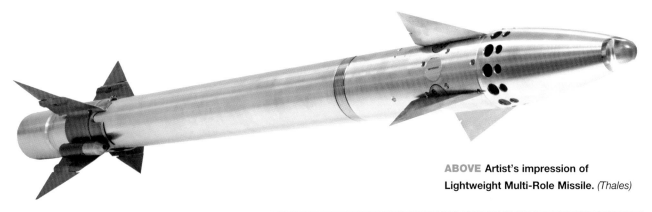

ABOVE Artist's impression of Lightweight Multi-Role Missile. *(Thales)*

by a fixed boost motor and, when this is expended, by a mid-body sustain motor. As the boost motor cannot be jettisoned, the sustain motor uses a downward-canted ventral nozzle. This arrangement offers better drop stability, maintains the centre of gravity in flight, avoids the safety issues associated with jettisoned motors and enables the data-link antenna to be incorporated at the rear of the missile.

There will also be a complementary alternative missile, the Lightweight Multi-Role Missile. Based on the Starstreak missile, this low-cost missile uses either laser beam-riding or semi-active laser guidance and will be carried in seven-cell 'snowflake' launchers that can attach to the pylons on either side of the Wildcat. It features a precision guidance system, allowing highly accurate targeting of a wide range of mobile targets, such as fast inshore attack craft and RIBs, out to ranges of about 8km.

Trainable decoy launcher

The current fixed DLH decoy launchers have the disadvantage that they may not present at the ideal elevation or azimuth angles for the

deployment of the decoy round, and that firing may be delayed, as they have no compensation for the rolling of the ship. A proposal to overcome these shortcomings is to replace the

ABOVE Artist's impression of Lynx Wildcat carrying two *Anti-Navire Léger* missiles on inboard pylons and 14 Lightweight Multi-Role Missiles in 'snowflake' configuration on the outboard pylons. *(AgustaWestland)*

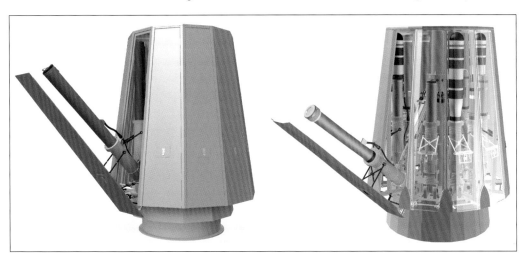

LEFT Trainable 12-barrel decoy launcher and cutaway. *(Chemring)*

RIGHT SeaRAM firing a rolling airframe missile. *(Raytheon)*

two DLH six-barrelled launchers by a trainable 12-barrelled launcher.

The new launcher can carry 130mm decoy rounds, each being stored behind a closure hinged at the bottom. When a firing solution is received the appropriate decoy is selected, the launcher rotates to the correct azimuth and the closure drops to bring the round to the ideal elevation. The barrel is stabilised in pitch, roll and azimuth until the decoy is fired towards the optimum position.

SeaRAM

A future alternative to the Phalanx CIWS Block 1B as the inner layer defence system is the SeaRAM with the Rolling Airframe Missile (RIM-116), so named because it is stabilised in flight by rotating about its longitudinal axis.

Based on the mounting and targeting systems of Phalanx, SeaRAM was developed to provide improved performance against supersonic sea-skimming anti-ship missiles. It can also engage helicopters and aircraft and is equipped with an 11-cell guided missile launching system, providing defence at more than double the range of Phalanx CIWS.

The Rolling Airframe Missile Block 1A missile (RIM-116B) incorporates an image-scanning seeker with the added capability of autonomous infrared all-the-way guidance to counter anti-ship missiles that do not employ on-board radar seekers. Enhanced digital signal processing provides increased resistance to countermeasures and improved performance in cluttered infrared background conditions. An advanced optical target detection device detects very low sea-skimming threats.

Although SeaRAM trials were undertaken on the destroyer HMS *York* in 2001, the option to fit the system was not pursued by the MoD. The attractiveness of SeaRAM may have been

SeaRAM RIM-116B Rolling Airframe Missile system		
Missile	Weight	13kg
	No carried	11
	Length	2.83m
	Diameter	120mm
	Wingspan	437.5mm
	Warhead	9.1kg blast-fragmentation
	Propulsion	Solid propellant rocket
	Range	9km
	Speed	700m/sec
	Autonomous guidance	Dual radar/infrared (all-the-way guidance)
Mounting	Above-deck weight	7,000kg (including missiles)
	Missiles carried	11
	Search radar	J-band 12 to 18 GHz, digital
	Track radar	12 to 18 GHz, pulse-Doppler, monopulse
	Secondary search	Forward-looking infrared 8 to 13μm
	Elevation	–10° to +80°
	Training	± 155°
	Working circle	3.5m
	Below-deck weight	714kg

increased in 2012 by further improvements introduced in the short production-run of Block 2 missiles (RIM-116C).

Valedictory remarks

The RN waited several decades for a replacement for the *Sheffield*-Class Type 42 destroyer. With the *Daring*-Class Type 45 destroyers they are now equipped with formidable and extremely advanced warships.

The destroyers incorporate an unprecedented level of innovative technology. Major new systems include the flexible and economic IEPS and their potent Sea Viper AAW system with its powerful Sampson MFR. Practically all the systems on the vessels demonstrate novel solutions to the problems and challenges of naval engineering and modern responses to traditional difficulties. Such innovation was not restricted to the destroyers alone. The techniques of manufacture and outfitting also broke new ground, as did the methods of prototyping, integrating and testing of the IEPS and combat systems. Many of these original processes were employed in the building of the *Queen Elizabeth* aircraft carriers and will carry forward to the Type 26 ASW frigates.

The advanced technology of a modern, complex warship like the Type 45 destroyer naturally entails a great degree of automation in the control of the weapons, propulsion and on-board service equipment. As a consequence, the full operation of these impressive vessels requires a ship's complement of only 191 – a reduction of more than 25% when compared to their smaller predecessors. Although fewer people are now required to handle more sophisticated and complex systems, it is undoubtedly vital to the performance of the destroyer that such personnel are of the highest calibre.

It is not only in areas of technology that the Type 45 destroyers represent new standards of excellence. Their accommodation is also a significant improvement on that of existing ships, and this newly established norm anticipates that to be adopted by other RN warships under development for the 21st century. The ship's facilities are designed for

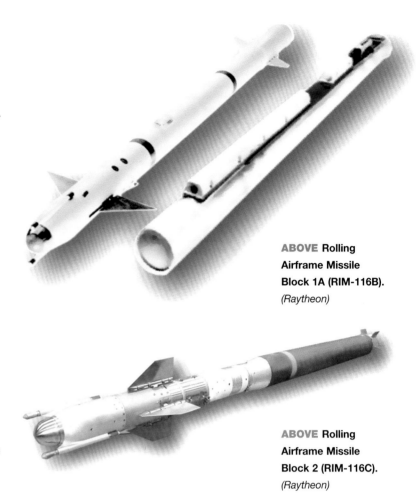

ABOVE Rolling Airframe Missile Block 1A (RIM-116B). *(Raytheon)*

ABOVE Rolling Airframe Missile Block 2 (RIM-116C). *(Raytheon)*

sailors of either gender. While accommodation on a warship will never be luxurious, each member of the ship's staff will have their own berth that is equipped for modern personal electronic devices.

The nature of technology and the unpredictable but inevitable changes to the threats that the RN faces means that the destroyers will have to change and evolve if they are to remain relevant to a modern navy. The unmatched flexibility and adaptability of the design will ensure that the destroyers can readily accommodate changes in technology. This will allow the warships to be modernised to ensure that their capabilities remain pertinent.

A highly capable warship is rather like a Formula 1 racing car that is ineffective without a talented driver. Despite the advanced technology, the efficacy of the Type 45 destroyers is nothing without that single most important factor: its well-led, trained and experienced ship's company.

Appendix 1

Glossary of naval and shipwright terms

Accommodation ladder A ladder suspended over the side of a ship to allow personnel to board the ship from boats (particularly when at anchor).

Aft Towards the *stern* of the ship.

Athwartships Orientated across the ship.

Ballast Heavy material stowed low in the ship to improve the vessel's stability.

Bilge The lowest part of the ship. It is the natural home of seawater that has leaked into the hull, and of liquids such as oil and detergent from tanks and equipment. This liquid is referred to as *bilge water* or just *bilge*.

Bollard A short, thick post (originally a short tree trunk) used for securing ropes and *hawsers*, especially lines used for mooring.

Bow The forward (pointed) part of the ship.

Brow The correct term for the 'gangway' linking the ship to the shore.

Bulkheads Upright partitions that are not part of the ship's hull.

Bulwark An extension of the hull above a weather deck, usually to form a protective barrier.

Cabins Sleeping accommodation of up to six bunks. Spaces with more than six bunks are termed *bunk spaces* or, if general-purpose living spaces, *messes*. All sleeping accommodation on Type 45 destroyers is in cabins.

Cable A rope securing the anchor (and any rope exceeding 80mm diameter); now also applied to electrical power cables.

Calorifier An electric water heater.

Capstan Rotating machine to haul in anchor chains, *hawsers* and the like.

Captain The Commanding Officer of a warship is formally called Captain, even though he or she may not hold the rank of captain. Most destroyer Commanding Officers hold the rank of Commander. The ship's company refer to the ship's Captain as *Father* or *The Old Man*. It is unclear if this will continue, as the first female Commanding Officer was appointed in 2012. Captains of commissioned ships are often synonymous with their ship – for instance, 'I must contact *Daring*.'

Citadel Core compartments of a warship that can be sealed and pressurised during action stations to prevent the penetration of harmful CBRN agents; access from compartments outside the citadel and the weather decks requires personnel to enter through an airlock or, if they have been exposed to contamination, through a cleansing station to remove any harmful agents before they enter the ship.

Coaming A raised watertight barrier that prevents water running into a cut-out in a deck such as a hatch or missile silo.

Compartment A generic term for a space between decks whose sides are bulkheads and, possibly, the ship's hull or the *superstructure*'s outer plating.

Con The action of directing the steering of the ship; this responsibility is passed to another officer (for instance the Officer of the Watch) with the phrase 'You have the con.'

Davit A small crane that can project over the side of the ship to hoist ship's boats and other items.

Deckheads The underside of decks seen from below.

Decks Horizontal surfaces. The *main deck* is the uppermost continuous deck and the highest deck of the hull. Decks below this are numbered sequentially 1, 2, 3 etc, and the decks above forming the *superstructure* are numbered sequentially 01, 02, 03 etc.

Ditch To discard material such as *gash* overboard.

Down-hand Working so that the work is beneath the worker rather than the more awkward position where the worker has to stretch up to weld or install items.

Down-take Air inlet trunking providing fresh air to diesels or gas turbines.

Drop anchor Lowering the anchor to the seabed to secure a ship.

Dry dock Dock that can be drained of water.

Eductor Type of pump with no moving parts. A stream of high-pressure water drawn past a nozzle enables fluids such as *bilge water* to be sucked from tanks connected to the nozzle.

Evolution A task, often to effect a new arrangement or disposition, requiring coordinated action for its successful completion.

Fairlead A small circular opening in the deck-edge or a ring-like structure on the deck to guide *cables* or *hawsers*.

Fighting the ship A term relating to the performance of offensive and defensive evolutions, dating from a period when such military duties were distinct from those of mariners, who were responsible for 'sailing the ship'.

Flare Term describing a ship's hull that increases width with height above the waterline.

Flats Open areas such as the *wardroom* or dining halls.

Flight deck Area designated for the landing and take-off of helicopters.

Fore/forward Towards the front of the ship.

Forecastle (pronounced *fo-c-sle*) The flat above the bow, so called because in Tudor ships this was a tall castle-like fighting platform.

Foremast See *masts*.

Frame Transverse strengthening of the ship's hull, analogous to a person's ribs, so often referred to as the ship's ribs. In wooden ships these were part of the hull's structure, which was then clad with wooden planks. Although modern warships are not constructed in the same way, frames are still key structural components. Frames are usually arranged at regular intervals along the length of the hull; the frame spacing of Type 45 destroyers is 0.7m.

Fuze A device to initiate the detonation of an explosive. Not to be confused with an electrical *fuse* that prevents high currents from causing damage.

Galley An area for the preparation of food (equivalent to a kitchen ashore).

Gash Rubbish or refuse, whence the term is also used for something surplus to requirements or useless.

General arrangement (GA) A diagram (generally printed A0 size) showing a plan of every deck and an elevation of the ship showing compartments. Although designers now use 3D models for their work, the GA is still a useful summary of the ship's layout.

Green seas (or green water) A solid wave of water coming aboard a ship.

Hatch An opening in a deck allowing access to a lower deck by means of a ladder. Hatches are surrounded by a *coaming*.

Hawser A thick cable or rope used in mooring or towing a ship, hence *hawse-pipe*, a pipe to lead a hawser or chain over the side.

Heads Toilets.

Hotwork Processes such as welding to join metal and flame cutting that become increasingly dangerous and disruptive as the build of the ship progresses.

Jackstay Wire cable between two ships to effect the transfer of supplies during replenishment at sea.

Jalousie A shutter having adjustable horizontal slats for regulating the passage of air.

Lobbies Small compartments opening off a *flat*.

Main passageway The central passageway, normally on the main deck and running the length of the ship.

Masts Tall, narrow (or in the case of the Type 45 foremast, not so narrow!) structures named in allusion to the masts that carry the sails of sailing ships. The large *foremast* carries the Sampson MFR, the small *main mast* the communications pole-mast and the *aft mast* the LRR. Where they are wide enough they, too, have decks, numbered as *superstructure* decks or, where they are not approximately the normal deck height (such as the highest aft-mast deck), with an alphanumeric (*eg* 04A).

Mezzanine deck (pronounced *mez-a-neen* deck) A term taken from mezzanine floors in architecture. On the Type 45 it is the balcony of a high space such as a machinery room or hangar.

Midships Situated in the central part of the ship.

Monitor (noun) Device for controlling the direction of a water jet in firefighting.

Moveable high-point A fixing used for replenishment at sea, where a line from the replenishing ship is attached to a ring at deck level (a sliding pad eye) on a trolley that is then hauled up the high-point track against the ship's *superstructure*.

Naval gunfire support Artillery bombardment of shore targets.

Pendant number (pronounced, and often misspelt, *pennant*) Letter and numbers identifying the type and unique number of a warship; HMS *Daring*'s pendant number is D32, where D indicates that it is a destroyer. Not to be confused with the two-letter deck code used by aircraft to identify their flight deck.

Plummer block A bearing used to support a propeller shaft.

Port The left-hand side of the ship when facing forward.

Pre-wetting Fine mist enveloping the ship to repel CBRN agents. The mist is generated by spraying seawater from superstructure nozzles.

Prime movers General term for engines such as gas turbines and diesel engines that provide the ship's propulsive and electrical power.

Quarterdeck The stern area of a ship's *weather deck* or space below the *flight deck*.

Radome Plastic dome covering a radar's antenna to protect it from the weather.

Redundant Components that are normally not required until the principal components fail, in which event they automatically take on the functions of the failed item. Dual redundant means that there is one fallback item, while triple redundant components have two fallbacks.

Reeve Process of hauling a rope through holes; now used for installing electrical cables that have to be reeved through a number of *bulkheads*.

Rig A term used for sets of sails but now principally used to describe uniforms or even clothing in general. The new No 4 rig (combat uniform) is, as is the way with bureaucracy, officially called a Personal Clothing System.

Screeve To mark a steel plate prior to cutting.

Scupper Any cunningly contrived orifice for the speedy removal of excess moisture – an opening, especially on the *weather deck*, that enables water to drain over the sides or into the *bilges*.

Shipwise During building, a description of a part of the ship that is in the correct orientation – for instance, a unit that has been fabricated upside down for ease of working is then turned 'shipwise' for further work.

Shipwright Someone whose occupation is to design, construct and repair ships; originally a hewer of wood.

Sickbay The place on board where a sailor can receive medical attention. In the days of sail sick-berths were located in the rounded stern that is in the shape of a bay, so sick-berths became sickbays.

Slipway A long inclined ramp on which the ship's hull is assembled and from which it is launched into the water.

Sonobuoy A disposable sonar device dropped by helicopters searching for submarines; its cylindrical main body floats on the sea's surface for a few hours, during which time it sends data back to the helicopter.

Soundings Measurements of the depth of water beneath the ship; now achieved by sonar, these were originally done by 'heaving (or swinging) the lead'.

Sponson For warships, a sponson is a protrusion from the hull to protect or to support equipment.

Stanchion Narrow post providing support for the guardrails or netting at the deck-edge.

Starboard The right-hand side of the ship when facing forward.

Stem The curve at the bow of a ship.

Stern The back, or *aft*, part of the ship.

Stowage Space for storage; 'stowing' implies storing in a neat and compact way.

Sullage Waste liquid and solids such as garbage, water contaminated with oil and spilt water from heads, bathrooms and galleys.

LEFT Sunset ceremony on HMS *Diamond*. With the alert of 'Sunset' the flag is lowered on the traditional command of 'Make it so!'. *(Crown Copyright, 2011 LA (Phot) Kyle Heller)*

Superstructure Part of the ship comprising the decks above the main deck that can extend the width of the ship but only run part of the length of the ship.

Top-hamper Term for weight carried high in the ship (originally sails and spars) that tends to make it heel over; it is a major factor in hull design.

Transceivers Communication or radar equipment containing both transmitters and receivers.

Transom The aftermost side of the hull.

Transverse activities Design factors that must be tackled on a whole-ship level. They have contributions from many of the ship systems and complex interactions between these systems must be taken into account. Examples are safety, survivability, services and overall electromagnetic compatibility.

Traveller block An encased pulley beneath which stores (or personnel in a boson's chair) are slung. The block is hauled between two ships by outhauls from each of them to effect transfers.

Up-take Trunking to extract exhaust gases from diesels or gas turbines by carrying them up the funnel.

Victuals (pronounced *vittles*) Food supplies and provisions for the ship's company, hence 'to victual' (take food on board the ship) and 'victualling' (supply of food).

Waist Middle part of the upper deck of a ship; originally because central section of sailing warships was lower than the forecastle or quarterdeck.

Wardroom The compartment where the officers eat. The term has now come to include the wardroom annex or anteroom where they relax and the officers' accommodation.

Watch system So that the warship may be operated around the clock, the ship's company is divided into two or more 'watches', with different watches performing duties ('on-watch') and being 'off-watch' at different times.

Weather deck A generic term for the uppermost decks of the ship that are exposed to the elements.

Weighing anchor Raising an anchor from the seabed and pulling it up to its stowed position against the side of the ship. The term derives from the time before mechanisation when sailors raised anchors by using their weight to turn a capstan.

Yardarm Originally a stout pole for carrying a sail, the term now applies to horizontal poles, usually projecting from masts, used to carry items such as anemometers or antennas that cannot be mounted close to the mast.

RIGHT While taking part in the removal of chemical weapons in Syria HMS *Diamond* undertakes replenishment at sea from the French auxiliary FS *Var*. *(French Navy Photo, 2014)*

Appendix 2

Abbreviations

2D Two-dimensional.
3D Three-dimensional.
AAW Anti-air warfare.
AC Alternating current.
ASCG Automatic small-calibre guns.
ASuW Anti-surface warfare.
ASW Anti-submarine warfare.
AWACS Airborne warning and control system.
CBRN Chemical, biological, radiological and nuclear (formerly NCBD).
CCTV Closed-circuit television.
CEC Co-operative engagement capability.
CESM Communications electronic support measures.
CIWS Close-in weapon system.
CMS Combat management system.
CO₂ Carbon dioxide.
CST Contractor's sea trials.
CW Chilled water.
DC Direct current.
DTS Data transfer system.
ECDIS Electronic Chart and Display Information System.
EHF Extra-high frequency.
EMPAR European multifunction phased array radar.
EOGCS Electro-optical gunfire control system.
EPMS Electrical power management system.
ESTD Electric ship technology demonstrator.
FICS Fully integrated communications system.
FoC First of Class.
FW Freshwater.
GmbH *Gesellschaft mit beschränkter Haftung*.
GPMG General-purpose machine gun.
GPS Global positioning system.

GRP Glassfibre reinforced plastic.
GT Gas turbine.
GTA Gas turbine alternator.
HADR Humanitarian aid and disaster relief.
HF High frequency.
HMA Helicopter Maritime Attack.
HMNB Her Majesty's Naval Base.
HMS Her Majesty's Ship.
HPSW High-pressure seawater.
HRH His/Her Royal Highness.
HVAC Heating, ventilation and air conditioning system.
IAP Incremental Acquisition Programme.
IEPS Integrated electric propulsion system.
IFF Identification friend or foe.
IMO International Maritime Organisation.
ISS *Internationale Schiff-Studien-GmbH* (International Ship Studies Co).
JTIDS Joint tactical information distribution system.
LF Low frequency.
LRR Long-range radar.
MARPOL International Convention for the Prevention of Pollution from Ships.
MARS Military Afloat Reach and Sustainability.
MCG Medium-calibre gun.
MdCN *Missile de croisière naval*.
METOC Meteorological and oceanographic.
MF Medium frequency.
MFR Multifunction radar.
MFS Medium-frequency sonar.
Mk Mark.
MoD Ministry of Defence.
Mod Modification.
NATO North Atlantic Treaty

Organisation.
NFR-90 NATO frigate replacement for the 1990s.
NM Nautical mile (UK) (=1.853km).
PAAMS Principal Anti-Aircraft Missile System.
PAF *Pilotage aérodynamique fort* (powerful aerodynamic control).
PIF *Pilotage d'interception en force* (interception thrust control).
PMS Platform management system.
RAF Royal Air Force.
RESM Radar electronic support measures.
RFA Royal Fleet Auxiliary.
RIB Rigid inflatable boat.
RM Royal Marines.
RN Royal Navy.
Satcoms Satellite communications.
SC Op Sonar control operator.
SCG Small-calibre gun.
SCOT Satellite communications on-board terminal.
SHF Super-high frequency.
SMART-L Signal multibeam acquisition radar for tracking, L-band.
SSGW Surface ship guided weapon.
SSTD Surface ship torpedo defence.
Sylver *Systeme de Lancement Vertical*.
TBM Theatre ballistic missile.
TBMD Theatre ballistic missile defence.
TLAM Tomahawk land attack missile.
TV Television.
UHF Ultra-high frequency.
UK United Kingdom.
USA United States of America.
USAF United States Air Force.
USN United States Navy.
USS United States Ship.
VHF Very-high frequency.
V/UHF Very/ultra-high frequency.
VUU Voice user units.

Index